The Simon and Schuster Listener's Guides
Edited by Alan Rich

OPERA

Alan Rich

Simon and Schuster
New York

A Quarto Book

A Fireside Book
Published by Simon and Schuster
A Division of the Gulf & Western Corporation
Simon & Schuster Building
Rockefeller Center
1230 Avenue of the Americas
New York, New York 10020

The *Listener's Guide* series was conceived and
edited by John Smallwood
Book design: Joan Peckolick
Design assistant: Elizabeth Fox
Text editors: Gene Santoro and Jane Dickler Lebow
Production: Millie Falcaro
Picture Research: Michelle Flaum

Produced and prepared by Quarto Marketing, Ltd.

Manufactured in the United States of America
Printed and bound by The Maple-Vail Manufacturing Group

Library of Congress Cataloging in Publication Data
Rich, Alan.
The Simon & Schuster listener's guide
to Opera
(A Fireside Book)
Includes discographies.
1.   Operas—Analysis, appreciation.
I.   Title.
MT95.R5   782.1   80-5077
ISBN 0-671-25442-1
ISBN 0-671-25443-X (pbk.)

Contents

Introduction

There is a well-known observation by Doctor Samuel Johnson that for over two centuries has gladdened the hearts of both the most avid opera-lover and the person who cannot stand a note of the stuff. "Opera," he wrote, "is an irrational and exotic entertainment." So it was in Dr. Johnson's time, and so it is today.

Neither the ardent admirer nor the horrified detractor can disagree on Dr. Johnson's "exotic." Music and drama —the two creative mainstreams that come together to form opera—are both capable of transporting us to any place at any time; Shakespeare and Tchaikovsky, each in his own way, can transport us to the Verona of Romeo and Juliet's time. Let these artistic forces—exotic drama and evocative music—work on each other, and the resultant hybrid's power to inspire the imagination is raised a millionfold. Through the exoticism of opera we may visit the haunts of Wagner's gods along the prehistoric Rhine, Dido's court at Carthage or the backwaters of Dr. Johnson's own London. We are swept into an empathy with the people of those times and places by the interaction of music and drama, enhanced by lights and costumes, scenery, and the opera house itself.

Dr. Johnson's other word was "irrational," and that takes more explaining. From the time when opera as we know it today was formally "invented" around the start of the seventeenth century to the present day, the whole of all great musical drama has been infinitely greater than the sum of its parts. The hostile outsider may regard opera as simply a play draped in attractive and relevant music, but the insider knows that it is a great deal more. The magic of opera is in the way that music and drama unite to create another art entirely. It's an art with its own language—and even its own time scale. If you try to think of opera simply as a kind of music, or of drama, you miss its essence.

It was always so. The first opera that the world regards as a masterpiece, Claudio Monteverdi's *L'Orfeo* of 1607, has as its text a dramatized version of the classic lyric legend: Orpheus the poet-singer, bereaved of his beloved Euridice, calling upon the eloquence of his music to gain entry to Hades and rescue her from the powers of darkness. On his journey, Orpheus encounters the surly boatman, Charon, who bars his entry to Hades. Orpheus serenades Charon with a song in several stanzas, and as he sings the orchestra sings, too: solo instruments from the ensemble—a violin, a trumpet, a harp—engage in a kind of fevered display of the art of music, wreathing the eloquence of the singer with eloquence of their own. Eventually, Charon is overcome. Monteverdi and his poet have given us not merely a dramatic argument, not merely a shower of musical virtuosity, but an operatic scene that takes both elements and elevates them into an undeniable artistic unity.

Another example of opera's uniqueness is the well-known Quartet in the last act of Giuseppe Verdi's *Rigoletto*, which was written in 1851—almost 250 years after *L'Orfeo*. Gilda, daughter of the court jester Rigoletto, has been seduced by her father's high-living employer, the Duke of Mantua. Rigoletto, in an effort to convince Gilda of the Duke's unworthiness, brings her to an inn where, through a window, she can spy on the Duke as he makes love to the sluttish Maddalena. The libretto was drawn from a Victor Hugo play, *Le Roi s'amuse*, in which the same scene occurs. Of course, in the play each character speaks in turn, whereas Verdi, through musical means, can create a different kind of story-telling by having all the characters involved sing about their feelings simultaneously. We hear, all at the same time, the Duke serenading Maddalena in a flowery ballad, Maddalena fending off his advances with flippant laughter, Rigoletto's stern admonitions to Gilda, and, above the other voices, Gilda's own heartbreak expressed in soaring, sobbing phrases. Music and drama have been combined here in a way that creates a different time sense from that of a play. The four characters can enact their parts simultaneously— in less time than would be needed in the spoken play— and each will still be clearly heard. On the other hand, the musical design of the piece stretches out the time elapsed, thus keeping the audience and singers happy with some agreeable musical and vocal elaborations and extending the time-scale.

Therefore, because the words-plus-music form of opera creates a level of intensity that can only relate to itself and because the composer's manipulation of time can often be totally unrelated to real time, opera could strike the outsider as irrational. Yet all art involves some suspension of rational thinking, some effort by the consumer to meet the creator of a work of art on his or her own level and in his or her own language. We are often required to accept the juxtaposition of incongruities. For example, we accept the Renaissance artist who uses the scenery of his own country and/or time as the background for the portrayal of totally unrelated events: a Mantegna sets his Gethsemane in the Tuscan hills, and Shakespeare populates the Athenian woods of *A Midsummer Night's Dream* with good Elizabethan workmen. If the painter and the playwright can violate the integrity of place, why must the operatic composer slavishly respect the integrity of time?

Opera has always inspired greater passions, both in its admirers and detractors, than any other art form. There are plenty of reasons for this: the grandeur of opera; the splendor of its presentation; the fact that, of all performing arts, opera is usually the most expensive—and the expense shows! However, the reason beyond all other reasons is simply this: opera is, above all, the glorification of the drama of the human voice at its expressive limits. We thrill to dancers or Olympic athletes who, after rigorous training, can extend their bodies in ways that we ordinary humans cannot; nobody can watch such an athlete or dancer without experiencing, somewhere in the subconscious, something of the same tug on the muscles. An operatic artist performs a similarly engrossing activity in acting out a drama by singing the words instead of merely speaking them—meanwhile straining (some would say distorting) the voice in order to produce a broader range of tone and of virtuosity than the normal speaking voice could encompass. This simply has to involve the audience's own response in what is going on: people who tell you that they can't stand opera "because of the shrieking" have simply refused to, or don't care to, accept its glorious quotient of irrationality.

There are, of course, many other aspects of opera that we must talk and write about, besides the basic fact of the voice. Some of them will form the substance of this book. Yet a crucial amount of what we can say—about the way Mozart brought the quality of humanness to operatic characters even when they were enmeshed in the artifice of an eighteenth-century plot; or about the way Wagner conceived of a "total art work" in which all the elements of music and theater combined into a mystic oneness—comes down eventually to the basic questions of who is singing the music, and how well that performance deals with the music, the words, and the way they go together to produce this incredible kind of art we call opera.

The aim of this book, as of all the books in this series of *Listener's Guides*, is to lead someone with the beginnings, at least, of a love for opera into a greater intimacy with a selected (if painfully short) group of some of the masterpieces in the field. A more or less historical outline will be followed, although there are times when that system will be more less and less more. Chapter 2, for example, is basically about the emergence of opera in Mozart's time, when there was an obvious breaking with the stylized dramatic subjects of an earlier era and the emergence of comedy and tragedy on a more human scale. It seems logical, despite the realities of chronology, to follow that trend as a continuous artistic line well into the nineteenth century, at least as far as Beethoven and Weber in Germany and the grand operas of Meyerbeer and Berlioz in France. That will mean, of course, that the next chapter will necessarily backtrack in time, because the bel canto style of Rossini was already sweeping Europe while Beethoven struggled with the final revisions on his *Fidelio.*

By the same token, the three chapters that cover the nineteenth century all spill into the twentieth, simply because composers have seldom been very cooperative with historians in adjusting their styles to the boundaries of years, decades, or centuries. These chapters (3, 4, and 5) also overlap one another in the time they cover, because the sociology of opera—the place it occupied in the cultural life of its country—became an important consideration in opera during and since the Wagnerian earthquake. It would be sheer academic peevishness to try to link in one chapter Wagner's *Tristan und Isolde,* Verdi's *La Forza del Destino,* and Berlioz's *Les Troyens,* simply because they were composed within two years of one another.

This brings up the ticklish problem of what the word *opera* really means. The word itself is no help: *opus* is simply the Latin word for "work," in the sense of a work of art, and *opera* is its plural. This bit of information clarifies nothing. Sometime during the first half-century of this newly created art form—although not at its very beginning—the word slithered into the vocabulary, where it remains. In most major cities today, the word *opera* immediately suggests what it did in Dr. Johnson's time: an exotic entertainment usually put on at irrationally high prices before an audience of bored and overdressed people. Even though the United States imported its first visiting troupe of operatic performers not long after the foundation of the Republic, generations of Americans have been brought up to regard a love of opera as something effeminate and hoity-toity—epitomized by the image of a pretentious nouveau-riche social climber who torments her down-to-earth husband by dragging him to the opera. The singer is invariably symbolized by a fat, armor-clad soprano shrieking discordantly, and everyone presumably sympathizes with the long-suffering man, who would rather be shooting pool.

Originally, the opera house in Italy came in all sizes, with budgets from meager to lavish, and the great Italian composers from 1650 to our own time were (and are) creating no more or less than their country's popular musical theater. Along with the masterworks of Verdi and the others, there were plenty of bad romantic Italian works that have long since disappeared, but at least there the artificial line that today has been drawn by arbiters of social respectability between the offerings of the opera house and those of the popular theater was then non-existent. Today we sometimes read that such-and-such a Broadway musical is considered by the critics "good enough to be an opera," a remark that means nothing and usually has the reverse effect of scaring people away. A century ago, in Italy, the composers who were comparable to the best on today's Broadway would have seen their works sharing the repertory with Verdi and Donizetti. To turn that around, we might say that Verdi would probably be writing for Broadway if he were alive today. The distinctions between one side of that line of social accep- tance and the other are, as often as not, expressible only in journalistic doubletalk.

Much of what this book attempts to cover, therefore, was, above all, the popular music theater of its place and its time. By that same token, the list extends into the popular musical theater of our own time, simply because it would be arbitrary not to do so.

I have put together this book with the assumption that anyone who picks it up already knows something about opera... if only the fact that it is a kind of theater where tenors and sopranos make passionate love to irrational if rather beautiful music, while mezzo-sopranos and bari- tones do everything in their power to break up the affair, and a bass pronounces words of wise judgment that nobody else listens to, and all the while an orchestra and chorus make some kind of background noise to drown out everything else. That is something of a simplification, of course, but not all that much.

In any case, I have made a few assumptions here just to keep this book at least nominally portable. I assume that you know where to find the complete plots of the operas discussed (Ernest Newman's *Stories of the Great Operas* for one, the same author's exhaustive books on Wagner, Edward Dent's *The Operas of Mozart,* Julian Budden's marvelous three-volume work on *Verdi,* Kobbe's *Complete Book of Operas* or, for that matter, the program notes that usually come with recordings). My own plot discussions will, therefore, often skimp certain areas, and concentrate instead on selected details to show how a specific composer deals in his own music with a specific moment in a plot. Each opera chosen will be discussed, therefore, not so much from an automatic compulsion to describe it in every nook and cranny of its hours-long course, but from the way the piece works as a distinctive blending of words and music to take its place as an opera.

Each operatic entry will be followed by a survey of available recordings: my own choices among complete recorded performances, in each case, but also important recordings of individual excerpts when such performances are memorable. At times, there may be recordings noted that are not currently in American catalogues but can be ordered in most large cities from the many good stores that handle imported records. Once in a while, there may even be mention made of a recording that has disappeared on both sides of the Atlantic. This is not meant as a form of torment, but as an incentive to enterprising collectors. Almost everybody interested in opera knows somebody with a record collection of virtually everything. If you don't know one, you can find one fairly easily: he'll be in the standing-room-only area of the nearest opera house, applauding (or booing) the loudest of anyone there. An irrational art demands irrational listeners.

1.
The
First Operas

During the last quarter of the sixteenth century, in Florence, Giovanni de Bardi, Count of Vernio, nobleman and noble patron of the arts, maintained one of the finest intellectual salons of the day. At this time, the Renaissance was at its creative floodtide, and Florence was the most fertile seed-bed of Renaissance humanism in Italy and the world. Bardi himself was descended from an old and distinguished banking family. He dabbled in philology, mathematics, neo-Platonic philosophy and the writings of that other great Florentine, Dante Alighieri. Above all, he dabbled in music, writing love songs and short dramatic dialogues that are, as dilettante exercises go, pretty good stuff.

At Bardi's home there regularly assembled, for several years beginning around 1576, a group of musicians and poets, diverse in the range of their talents and interests but united in at least one regard. This group—which called itself the Camerata—was motivated by a desire to create a new art form, one in which music and poetry would join to create an artistic expression higher than either element by itself. They believed that the music of their own time had lost its power to express poetry—most of all, because the gnarled complexity of the madrigal and related song forms made it impossible to hear words clearly. One member of the Camerata, a composer named Vincenzo Galilei, formulated the purpose of the group in a monograph entitled *The Dialogue between Old and New Music*, published in 1581.

The thrust of the argument was that music, currently awash in artifice, should return to the direct expression that typified the drama of ancient Greece, an argument that cropped up more than once in the history of musical drama. It did not matter that beyond a few fragments of theoretical writing, the Florentine aesthetes knew nothing about the actual music of Periclean Athens. It was enough that they suspected that the great lyric dramas of Sophocles and Euripides were chanted rather than spoken and that the nature of the chants was tied to a complicated ethical system in which specific harmonies had specific moral implications: one type of harmony for manliness, another for amorous passion, and so forth.

There had, of course, been musical drama of a sort since the time of the Greeks. More and more medieval manuscripts turn up, as scholars ferret out the contents of monastery attics and basements, to indicate that the message of the Church was often carried out in the form of acted-out sung drama, often of considerable extent. We have marvelous modern reconstructions of some of this music, notably the twelfth- or thirteenth-century *Play of Daniel* from the Abbey of Beauvais, in which the story of the Handwriting on the Wall and of Daniel in the Lions' Den is chanted by singers portraying the various characters, and with the accompaniment of instruments of one kind or another. In the sixteenth century, in fact, another kind of sung drama became popular for a while shortly before the Camerata made its pronouncement: the Venetian "Madrigal-Comedy" in which a story was acted out in pantomime while the words of the characters were sung by a small ensemble of madrigal singers off to the side. Yet the very fact that this music was sung in counterpoint, and, therefore, that the words were often lost in the complex texture of the music, lent force to the arguments advanced by the members of Count Bardi's circle of intellectuals.

From among the membership in the Camerata, two composers at least, Giulio Caccini and Jacopo Peri, joined with the poet Ottavio Rinuccini and, around the turn of the century, produced a series of dramatic works in which stories from classic mythology were enacted, with the characters singing in a continual solo melody supported by a keyboard instrument and possibly reinforced by one or two stringed instruments. During carnival season or at festive occurrences, these "dramatic fables," "dramas through music," or "musical fables" were given in Florence on small stages in one or another nobleman's palace, and they achieved a measure of popularity. Heard today, as one or two occasionally are, these early works may seem a little lacking in emotional resonance. Yet, the qualities that most attracted their composers at the time, particularly the way the harmonies are struck to underscore the words of passion in the text, retain a great deal of power even today.

The idea soon spread. Vincenzo Gonzaga, Duke of Mantua, heard Peri's *Euridice* in Florence and determined to have musical drama in his own palace. He commissioned the greatest Italian composer of the day, Claudio Monteverdi, to create a work for Mantua, and the reward, in 1607, was *L'Orfeo*, the first authentic masterpiece in the genre. In 1608 Monteverdi's pupil, Marco da Gagliano, created another work for Mantua, *La Dafne*, using a Rinuccini text that had already been set to music by several Camerata members. In the score of Gagliano's *La Dafne* we encounter, for the first time in musical history, the word *opera*.

Within a few years, the fame of the new musical theater had spread throughout Italy, and particularly to Venice. In that city there had long been a fondness for a kind of musical drama that predated actual opera by some years: the madrigal-comedy, a long series of polyphonic madrigals that would be linked together to follow a dramatic text. The story itself was usually enacted in pantomime—as opposed to the genuine operatic form, in which there was no separation between dramatic action and music. Yet the madrigals themselves, especially in the hands of such major composers as Adriano Banchieri, were of high quality, and the plots, which often involved burlesque or satire, attracted large audiences.

Thus, Venice had something of a ready-made audience for the new art form. In 1638 the first public opera house, the Teatro Tron di San Cassiano, was opened there, and by 1680 Venice alone had no fewer than eight public opera houses. Monteverdi was lured to Venice, where he composed his last operatic masterpiece, *The Coronation of Poppea*. A native Venetian, Francesco Cavalli, composed no fewer than forty-one operas, many of which were performed all over Europe during his lifetime. Much of Cavalli's music has been restored to circulation in the past few years.

What was all this music like? It took very little time for Italy's operatic composers to sense the tastes and desires of a public no longer consisting of a nobleman and his guests, but rather a crowd of ticket-buyers of no particular pedigree. Already, in Monteverdi's *L'Orfeo*, the austere musical recitation of the Camerata had been tempered with episodes of more musical design: madrigalesque choruses, overtly melodic songs, and dances. The shrewdest Venetian composers, Cavalli among them, devoted much of their energy to writing vocal music that was attractive to the crowd and also fitted the vocal talents of singers. Cavalli's operas which, like most works of the time, were based on classic legends, were keenly planned to include comic scenes and, even more important, songs in which a favored soprano or tenor could show off before a crowd of fervent admirers. In fact, it is reasonably safe to assert that operatic society, as it exists today on both sides of the footlights, was born in Venice during the great operatic years of the mid-seventeenth century.

But Venice wasn't the only operatic center. By 1680 almost every Italian city boasted at least one house, and the prosperous southern metropolis of Naples teemed with activity that rivalled that at Venice. The prolific

Alessandro Scarlatti, born in 1660, composed his first opera at the age of 19. He is known to have composed more than 115 full-length operas altogether, although many scores have been lost. Even so, the melodic grace of the best Scarlatti operas, and the fantastic display possibilities suggested in the music, reveal a musical society in Naples that could support opera on a high artistic level.

By 1680 much of the paraphernalia that was to remain with opera for nearly two centuries had taken shape. The basic plan of a work was as follows: the story would be carried forward mostly in the recitative, in which music that closely followed the rhythm of the words would be sung by a character with the lightest kind of accompaniment. In the ensuing aria the form and progress of the music was governed more by purely musical considerations: shapely, easily recognizable tunes, a formal arrangement in which the tune would return, usually much embellished by the singer with improvised trills, roulades and the like, and, quite often, an even longer spot for improvisation, a cadenza, near the end. (When the composer failed to provide his singer with a cadenza, the enterprising performer usually stuck one in anyhow.) The aria, as the more lyric, formal part of the opera, was usually contemplative in tone. In other words, a singer might carry an action forward in recitative, and wonder why she or he had done so in the following aria. It sounds like a fairly inflexible arrangement, but it worked to the satisfaction of huge audiences.

Opera quickly spread outside Italy, too. By 1650 Italian operatic troupes were regularly journeying northward, carrying with them the great machinery by which stunning stage effects were accomplished: a descent of gods from the heavens or an earthquake or two always impressed audiences. In Paris Louis XIV was enthralled with his Italian visitors, and a young man from one troupe, aware of a good thing, offered his services to the king as director of his own company. This young man was Giovanni Battista Lulli, who honored his new patron by Frenchifying his name to Jean-Baptiste Lully. At Louis's court Lully turned out French operas, inspired by the Italian manner but cleverly incorporating the one element dearest to the heart of Louis himself, the dance. Lully's even greater successor was a native Frenchman, Jean-Philippe Rameau, who created for Louis XV a series of operatic works including several tragedies of exceptional melodic beauty, as well as the fantastic hybrid *Les Indes Galantes*—half opera, half ballet, all spectacle.

Even farther to the north, the Italian operatic style reached England in the work of that country's first great composer, Henry Purcell, whose one true opera, the brief but ravishingly beautiful *Dido and Aeneas,* seems to revive the intense emotionality of Monteverdi. Much else by Purcell, even though not strictly opera, has a strong operatic flavor and shows a mingling of the composer's own artistic bravado with a quasi-Italian feeling for the voice: sets of songs, choruses, and incidental pieces for dozens of minor British plays that otherwise would surely have been forgotten by now.

Yet England's finest composer of Italian opera was a German, George Frideric Handel, who spent early years in Italy soaking up the essence of the Neapolitan style and went on to write better Neapolitan operas than Alessandro Scarlatti himself. By the time Handel was ready for his first voyage to London, in 1711, he found the town ripe and ready for its own Italian opera. The town was, if anything, a willing operatic colony of Naples. No matter that its self-appointed moral guardians, essayists Joseph Addison and Richard Steele, railed almost weekly in their periodical, the *Spectator,* against the lunacy of self-indulgent singers serenading Londoners in some foreign tongue while the stage around them teemed with trained monkeys and birds, goddesses recumbent and castrated male singers rampant. The Italian madness was to continue, with Handel as its newly installed leader (and, at least, creating better works than his rivals) until a day in January 1728 when the bubble suddenly burst.

The needle was applied in a work by another transplanted German, Johann Pepusch, set to a text by John Gay, an Englishman. It was called *The Beggar's Opera,* and its greatest achievement was to hold the mirror of satire up to the excesses of Italian opera and cause London to look into that mirror. Opera was not murdered in London by *The Beggar's Opera:* it merely went into a time of decline wherein its lesser composers slunk away, and Handel himself pondered alternatives—which he later put into practice.

Actually, the desire to refine some of the artificialities out of the ego-encrusted Italian form of opera was not merely a London phenomenon. Not many years after *The Beggar's Opera,* the composer Christoph Willibald Gluck, who had been writing some fair copies of Italianate models for Viennese audiences, also came to realize that the excessive pandering to virtuosos and their fan clubs, among other abuses, had robbed a potentially noble art of its dramatic power. In 1767 Gluck included, with the publication of his opera *Alceste,* a preface calling for a reform of opera. Specifically, he called for an end to pandering to singers, for strict adherence to what the composer put into his score and nothing else, and for a return to simplicity so that music could be used to enhance the passion of words—to the direct expression that typified the drama of ancient Greece. This challenge in the name of quality accompanied the very invention of opera. One hundred eighty years later Gluck recognized the need to sound this challenge again.

Claudio Monteverdi *(1567-1643)*

L'Orfeo. *Musical fable in five acts; libretto by Alessandro Striggio. First performance, Mantua, February 1607*

Claudio Monteverdi

The fable of Orpheus, whose sweet singing charmed gods and mortals alike and who, deprived of his beloved Euridice, descends to Hades to beg for her return, was the subject most often used by the first generation of operatic composers. And why not? What greater testimonial could there be to the power of words and music than the central scene of the legend, wherein Orpheus must summon every jot of his lyric talent to gain admission to the forbidden realm ordinarily barred to all but the dead?

Monteverdi was already known throughout Italy as a supremely gifted composer of madrigals and sacred music when he was commissioned in 1607 by the Duke of Mantua to try his hand at the music-drama that had been invented a decade before in Florence. Monteverdi had been attracted by this rather new representational style but seems to have instinctively recognized its limitations: continued unrhythmic recitation above the simplest musical support, however expressive, would soon lose appeal for its audiences.

He asked for, and received, musical forces of unprecedented size for the time: soloists, a chorus, and a varied assemblage of instruments with which to form what was to be music's first real orchestra. No previous composer had set down on paper specifications for exact instrumentation: so many strings here, brass and small organ to underscore the mystery of Hades, higher-pitched brass for the triumphal ending. The result is more than a marvelous, extraordinarily moving musical setting of the great legend: it is a remarkable synthesis of past, present, and future musical styles, created at a moment in artistic history that Monteverdi himself must have recognized as crucial.

To ears accustomed to the relative lushness of later opera, Monteverdi's music for *L'Orfeo* may sound rather thin at first. Much of it is delivered in a flexible, non-rhythmic melodic line, discreetly supported by the keyboard instrument (harpsichord or organ), with a few stringed instruments to provide additional color. But as you rehear this music, you find how closely it follows the passion of the text, and how fluid melodic lines take dramatic shape from the harmonies that underlie them. Beyond this, there was Monteverdi's own keen sense of drama, in which orchestral interludes, dances, and choruses were interspersed for the sake of both musical and dramatic variety.

The emotional impact of Monteverdi's score remains vivid today. The scene in which Orpheus importunes the boatman Charon to ferry him across the River Styx to Hades, with the orchestral instruments joining the ardor of the singer's song, is spellbinding. However, the dramatic climax in this treatment of the story occurs earlier, when the mysterious Messenger must intrude upon the gathering of Orpheus and the shepherds with the dire news that Euridice has died. Orpheus himself is speechless at first; two shepherds must speak for him until he recovers, and then they echo the Messenger's revelation. Then Orpheus must speak, although still somewhat numbed: "Thou art dead, and I live...." Listen, then, as the music gathers emotional power to its great climax: "Farewell, Sun; farewell Sky; and Earth, farewell." Note, too, that by reversing the word order for the third "farewell," the poet allows the composer to come down from his dramatic climax on that final "addio."

Later operas, notably the well-known *Orfeo ed Euridice* of Gluck, resolve the tragic legend by restoring Euridice to life a second time after the backward glance from Orpheus has caused her to fall. (Only in a little-known opera by Haydn does Orpheus meet the fate of returning to Earth and being torn apart by Maenads, as told in the legend.) Here Striggio's drama leaves Euridice to die, with Orpheus taken to Heaven by Apollo and installed as a star close to his beloved for all eternity.

Selected Recordings

L'Orfeo

Magali Schwarz, Eric Tappy, and Wally Staempfli, with Michel Corboz and the Lausanne Vocal and Instrumental Ensemble *(RCA)*

Cathy Berberian, Lajos Kozman, and Rotraud Hausmann, with Nikolaus Harnoncourt and the Concentus Musicus of Vienna *(Selecta/Telefunken)*

Both performances use instruments that are either survivors from Monteverdi's own time or, more likely, newly built to ancient specifications, bringing up the age-old problem of authenticity at all costs *versus* intelligent compromise. As with all his recorded performances, Harnoncourt shows himself to be an unquestioned authority on Baroque performance practice; his instruments buzz and chirp and project a marvelous sense of historic distance. Do they, at the same time, project a sense of the grandeur of this music? I think not. There is somewhat more life and substance in the Corboz performance, although again, the disposition of instruments follows Monteverdi's own specifications. However, Corboz seems to be saying—rightly—that no music could survive if even the great masterpieces were intended to sound dull. A slavish rendering of the specifications laid down by a composer in 1607 will not work well when the listeners that it is aimed at have heard Beethoven, Wagner, and Alban Berg. Beyond this, there is the finely expressive singing, on the Corboz recording, of Eric Tappy, a most moving Orpheus, and of Wally Staempfli, as Music herself, in the opera's prologue.

Henry Purcell *(1659-1695)*

Dido and Aeneas. *Opera in three acts; text by Nahum Tate. First performance, London, December, 1689*

Henry Purcell

Clearly under the spell of the operas he heard during his studies in Italy, Purcell turned out reams of dramatic music during his brief lifetime, including some sets nearly extensive enough to pass as operas (for example, nearly three hours of superlative songs, choruses, and dances to go with *The Fairy Queen,* a thoroughly hacked-up paraphrase of *A Midsummer Night's Dream*). Actually, Purcell's only real opera— in the sense of a work that can stand alone on its dramatic substance—is *Dido and Aeneas,* a work that would be of no consequence except for the sublimity of its music. It seems to have been commissioned to be sung by the students of Josiah Priest's Boarding School for Girls in London. We know neither why anyone would hire Purcell to do this nor who sang the male roles, but we do know that it was performed once at the school. Beyond that, there is the libretto of Nahum Tate to contend with, with its slangy rhymes and rhythms that Purcell still managed to set expressively.

However, Purcell could not supply what the text simply omitted: any real definition of the wandering Trojan Aeneas who, after falling in love with Queen Dido and living it up at her court in Carthage, is compelled by a ruse to forsake his beloved and follow the call of duty to Rome. Aeneas shuffles in and out of the opera as a shadow: even the sailor who, at the start of Act III, is given a boozy yo-ho-ho song to sing, is more fully identified as to character.

By contrast, the figure of Dido is far from cloudy: she dominates the short opera as she must have dominated Purcell's own imagination. If Monteverdi's *L'Orfeo* was the first great opera, Purcell's Dido was the first great operatic role—the more remarkable in a work lasting no more than an hour. From the moment of her first entry, confessing in broken rhythms and melodious sighs that she is "press'd with torment," she is made by Purcell's music into a character of towering grief. Even the song about this grief, sung later on by Dido's confidante Belinda ("Oft she visits this mountain...") has a throb that takes its force from Dido herself.

The final lament, as the abandoned Dido bids farewell to Belinda and begs her, "Remember me, but ah! forget my fate," will stop a hearer's breath when properly sung. The musical design is astonishing. Underlying the aria is a repeating four-bar phrase, a descending chromatic figure in the lower strings, but the vocal line breaks free of this regularity and soars across musical boundaries. As the lament ends—and if there is applause here it has been poorly sung—the commenting chorus closes the opera on a sad quatrain with music so simple, so quiet that it resembles merely the fall of a last leaf from a winter-stricken tree.

Selected Recordings

Dido and Aeneas

Janet Baker, Raimund Herincx, and Patricia Clark, with Anthony Lewis and the St. Anthony Singers and English Chamber Orchestra *(L'Oiseau Lyre/Decca)*

Janet Baker, Peter Pears, and Norma Burrowes, with Steuart Bedford and the Aldeburgh Festival Ensemble *(London/Decca)*

Josephine Veasey, John Shirley-Quirk, and Helen Donath, with Colin Davis, the John Alldis Choir, and the Academy of St. Martin-in-the Fields *(Philips)*

Kirsten Flagstad, Thomas Hemsley, and Elisabeth Schwarzkopf, with Geraint Jones and the Mermaid Theatre Company *(World Records/EMI)*

The luxury of choice here is spectacular: the first two selections are readings of extraordinary majesty by Janet Baker—the only differences being the quavery Aeneas of Peter Pears versus the undramatic Raimund Herincx and the use, on the Baker-Pears recording, of an edition of the score that was rather fussed over by Benjamin Britten. The performance under Colin Davis, with the splendid work of Veasey and Shirley-Quirk, does, therefore, press the first Baker version rather strongly. Then there is the splendid old Flagstad performance, with the young Schwarzkopf's limpid Belinda, dating from the performances (done somewhat as a lark) that reopened London's restored Mermaid Theatre in 1951. Whatever language Flagstad and Schwarzkopf may be singing (a matter open to some dispute), the rolling eloquence of the older soprano and the brightness of the younger are virtually irresistible. The recording is somewhat faint; still, this is one of those essential records, for irrational but potent reasons.

George Frideric Handel *(1685–1759)*

Rodelinda. *Opera in three acts; text by Antonio Salvi, adapted by Nicola Haym. First performance, London, February 1725*

George Frideric Handel

Purcell's operas and near-operas had given the English public a taste for musical drama in the Italian manner, translated and otherwise adapted to the English language. However, by the time Handel arrived in London in 1710, London had totally succumbed to Italian opera in Italian, and the staid Londoners had become an operatic public whose passions for the music and its singers and capacity for the most absurd anti-dramatic spectacle staged in the name of opera, rivalled the most avid claques in Italy.

Handel's operatic career reached its artistic peak during the years 1720–28, when he served as one of three directors of the Royal Academy of Music, London's most splendid opera house. Here he composed Italianate opera of extraordinary variety, richer and more elegant in tone than even that of his Italian-born co-director and great rival Giovanni Bononcini. His operas for the Academy ranged widely in substance. In *Giulio Cesare* there was the music of love (Caesar and the alluring Cleopatra, of course) and of war; *Tamerlano* plumbed the essence of tragedy; *Riccardo Primo* included a storm scene of amazing power.

Rodelina dates from 1725 and forms, with the earlier *Giulio Cesare* and *Tamerlano,* the high-water mark of Handel's time at the Academy. Its romantic plot, set in ancient Lombardy, is the kind of romantic farrago that might just as well have served Verdi 150 years later: a villainous pretender to the throne has banished the rightful king, abetted by the banished king's sister, to whom he (the pretender) is betrothed. Rodelinda, the suffering wife of the banished king, is meanwhile wooed by the pretender. All comes out as hoped for: the rightful king is rescued and reunited with his chaste and faithful Rodelinda, and the traitors are punished as they deserve.

Static—even, at times, silly—as plots of this genre are, they served the talents of the great composers of the day quite beautifully. Handel's music for *Rodelinda* is remarkable for its emotional range; if your knowledge of the composer's music is limited to his *Messiah,* the poignance of the music—for example, Rodelinda's sublime lament near the end of Act II, or the invocation to Nature sung by the banished king, in which the orchestral instruments are marvelously used to imitate the murmurs of forest and brook—will astound you.

Handel's operas lay neglected for much of this century, but now more frequent revivals are taking place. You must be prepared to accept certain conventions of the time that, even within the irrationality of opera, may be difficult to take. In *Rodelinda,* for example, many of the major male roles were, in Handel's time, allotted to *castrati* and must today be sung by contraltos (whose figures may or may not look convincing in masculine garb). The extraordinary beauty of the music should be enough to atone for these violations of realism.

Three years after the success of *Rodelinda,* Handel's time at the Royal Academy came to an end. The taste for Italian extravagance had simply run its course, and the enormous success of that most devastating lampoon, *The Beggar's Opera* (discussed later in this book) hastened the demise of the academy's profligate productions. Nevertheless, Handel continued to write operas, although many of them were mounted on a smaller scale. The famous "Largo," the first piece by Handel that most of us learn, is actually an aria from one of the later operas, *Serse.* Hard as it may be to believe, this "Largo" was actually intended as a satire, a love song sung by Xerxes, King of Persia—to a tree.

Selected Recordings
Rodelinda
   Teresa Stich-Randall, Maureen Forrester, Helen Watts, and Alexander Young, with Brian Priestman and the Vienna Radio Orchestra *(Westminster)*
   (Aria, *"Dove sei, amato ben?)*
   Kathleen Ferrier (in English as "Art Thou Troubled?") *(London)*
   Janet Baker *(Philips/Phonogram)*

Although there is only one recording of the complete *Rodelinda,* as opposed to other Handel operas that have been recorded several times, the performance under Priestman is a rare instance of that fine blend of respect for style and the power to communicate deep emotion. The singers are finely trained to honor the bounds of the Baroque singing style: the complex language of ornamentations over certain notes to enhance their intensity, the subtle slowing-down as a piece nears its end. Yet Priestman is splendidly able to create a living document rather than a museum piece. Then there is that one splendid aria, sung by the exiled King Bertarido, which is one of the most ravishing melodies ever penned. Kathleen Ferrier, who died of cancer in 1953 after a career that lasted less than a decade, sang this aria in a soupy English translation, but with a voice and manner of heartbreaking majesty. Her recording belongs in the collection of anyone who values what the voice can do. Janet Baker, singing the Italian original in a more stylistically accurate version, provides yet another version of this aria that must rank as sublime.

Jean-Philippe Rameau *(1683–1764)*

Les Indes Galantes. *Opera-ballet in a prologue and four entrées; text by Louis Fuzelier. First performance, Paris, March 1736*

Jean-Philippe Rameau

Opera had come to France when the Italian-born Lully won favor at the court of Louis XIV in the 1670s, but it would be a half-century after Lully's death before one of France's native sons achieved the same measure of success. That turned out to be Rameau, who was already well known as a composer of elegant church music and keyboard pieces when, in 1733, he had his first dramatic success with his *Hippolyte et Aricie,* a lyric tragedy drawn from the *Phèdre* of Racine. As any French composer had to be, Rameau was a keen observer of the two greatest influences in French taste: the theater and the dance. From his studies in theater, he arrived at a flexible way of setting French speech rhythms to music—not the Italianate recitative, and not the mellifluous Italian aria, but something in between. At the same time, his vocal writing managed to sustain a rhythmic outline that constantly echoed the favorite dance steps of the day, and the action of even his most tragic operas breaks off constantly to allow the corps de ballet its time in the spotlight.

This simple, elegant, highly ornamented kind of vocal writing is distinctly different from the earlier, more convoluted, somewhat more deeply colored Baroque style. Like the fanciful decorations of a Boucher or a Fragonard painting, this elegant musical manner is often spoken of as "rococo."

Les Indes Galantes dates from 1736, although three of its four acts had been given a year before. It is a strange and wonderful hybrid, designed to solve no dramatic problems but to please almost every kind of audience. It was Rameau's most successful opera during his lifetime, and a revival in pure *ancien-régime* luxury at the Paris Opéra in 1952 was one of the greatest hits in that company's two-hundred-year existence.

The plot is simply told: a group of squabbling lovers are sternly lectured to by the Goddess of Love, who then stages four exotic demonstrations of the power of *l'amour.* One takes place in a Turkish harem, where a captive maiden is rescued by her true-love; one takes place among the Incas of Peru, where a hopeless impasse is solved by a volcanic eruption; and the two succeeding acts take place in a Persian flower garden and among some North American Indians. The opera contains less singing than it does dancing and spectacle, but everything is wonderfully colored by Rameau's attempt to create exotic and indigenous songs and dances.

Selected Recordings

Les Indes Galantes
    Jean-Claude Malgoire and La Grande Ecurie et la Chambre du Roi *(Columbia)*
    (Excerpts) Maurice Hewitt and a Vocal and Orchestral Ensemble *(Vox)*

Malgoire's complete version is excellent in all respects, and his group of singers includes the veteran Jeanine Micheau as the Indian girl who prefers her noble-savage lover to both the Spanish or French officers who are courting her. The entire singing ensemble is beautifully trained in the ornate French style, and Malgoire's orchestra is enhanced by the presence of rather nicely played reconstructions of instruments of Rameau's own time. The ancient Hewitt recording, one of the first long-playing records ever made (and probably hard to locate), has one great asset, the singing of the eloquent Camille Mauranne as the Inca Sun-Priest who, thwarted in his love for the Peruvian princess, hurls himself into the erupting volcano. Honest!

Christoph Willibald Gluck *(1714–1787)*

Orfeo ed Euridice, *opera in three acts; text by Ranieri Calzabigi. First performance, Vienna, October, 1762; revised French version, first performance, Paris, August 1774*

Orfeo ed Euridice

The first opera discussed in this book, Monteverdi's *L'Orfeo,* came about as the consequence of an attempt by composers and poets to create a dramatic form that would honor the spirit of true drama. The subject matter, the story of Orpheus using the power of music to overcome the forces of evil, accorded with the spirit of reform that initiated both the Baroque era and the institution of opera.

Now, more than 150 years later, here is another composer, the Austrian-born Gluck, already a successful composer of several operas in the artificial Italian tradition, again signalizing a reform, a return to musical drama that was to concentrate on pure dramatic meaning. Once again, the subject matter is the story of Orpheus and his lute, overcoming through the power of music the Furies who would deny to him the return of his beloved Euridice.

Gluck's obsession was to "purify" opera by cleansing it of the domination of egoistic singers. He demanded that his singers perform only what he had written in the score, without embellishment or interpolated cadenzas. Instead of the artifice of the closed-form aria in which action could not go forward, he developed a more flowing musical style in which recitative and aria blended as a continuous expressive line. Orchestra and chorus became integral parts of the drama, rather than mere supports to keep the music going while the singers caught their breath.

Gluck's *Orfeo ed Euridice* begins with a fine illustration of his hopes for a drama heightened by its music. At the fresh grave of Euridice, the chorus sings a solemn, slow-moving lament, as spare and poignant as the chorus that ends Purcell's *Dido and Aeneas*. The grieving Orpheus interrupts with a haunting cry, nothing more than the name of his departed beloved. The scene draws its power from its utter simplicity. Later on, however, there is an even more memorable moment, as Orpheus approaches the gates of Hades and seeks entry. Ever more passionate grows his plea, as the stern "No" of the guardian Furies becomes softer and softer. Finally, the chorus parts to soft, melting harmonies, and the power of music as persuader has triumphed.

Even the dancing in *Orfeo ed Euridice*—much of which was created for the later, Paris version—is more than mere decoration. The dances in Elysium—where the souls of the blessed abide after death—are devised to contrast extremely with the darkness outside, and the famous slow dance, with its flute solo, remains one of the most haunting melodies of its time. The ultimate distillation of the lyric power of Gluck's opera, however, is the great aria near the end, when Euridice forces Orpheus to break his vow not to look upon her, and she dies a second time. "Che farò senz' Euridice?" ("What shall I do without Euridice?") sings the desperate lover, and the utter chastity of the music draws our tears.

Selected Recordings

Orfeo ed Euridice

Marilyn Horne, Pilar Lorengar and Helen Donath, with Sir Georg Solti and the Royal Opera House Orchestra *(London/Decca)*

Kathleen Ferrier, with Charles Bruck and the chorus and orchestra of Radio Nederland *(EMI)*

Dietrich Fischer-Dieskau, Gundula Janowitz, and Edda Moser, with Karl Richter and the Munich Bach Orchestra *(Deutsche Grammophon)*

Current tendencies are to perform *Orfeo ed Euridice* in a hybrid of the original Viennese and later Parisian versions

—using the contralto (originally, of course, a male alto) and the Italian text from Vienna but adding the ballets and the Elysian Fields aria composed later for Paris. This is a reasonable compromise, but it might be more interesting to hear an entire Paris version, with the role of Orpheus rewritten for a tenor. Such a recording, with Leopold Simoneau as Orpheus and the late Hans Rosbaud conducting, was formerly available on Philips and might still be found.

Failing this, the marvelous tension of Horne's performance, although somewhat driven by Solti, is hard to resist, and the eloquence of the Fischer-Dieskau performance (singing the Vienna version an octave lower) is also a stirring experience. Then there is also the overpowering performance by Kathleen Ferrier, who in her tragically short career learned to mirror in her rich and plangent voice every shade of Gluck's sorrowing hero. The recording has been pieced together from a broadcast performance made in the Netherlands in 1952, when Ferrier already knew she was dying of cancer. Neither the supporting cast nor the conducting are worthy of the sovereign work of Ferrier; yet the miracle is that the performance exists at all, and it cannot be passed over.

John Christopher Pepusch *(1667–1752)*

The Beggar's Opera, *opera in three acts; text by John Gay. First performance, London, January 1728*

usic may, as Shakespeare put it, be the food of love; yet the remarkable history of *The Beggar's Opera* suggests that music can also serve as a weapon of devastation—at least in the hands of the proper marksman. John Gay (1685–1732) was one of these. He was a minor writer in London, a friend of the great satirist Jonathan Swift but not otherwise in much favor in high circles. It was probably Swift who first suggested to Gay that he vent his spleen on London's corrupt aristocracy in the form of poetry—a sheaf of songs and verses in English set in the high-flown manner of the time but declaimed by thugs and other low-life types instead of the gods and classic heroes dear to the hearts of the upper class and royalty.

This was the time of Handel's great operatic popularity, yet it was also a time when London's more intellectual circles were becoming fed up with the artifice of contemporary opera, with its stilted plots and its dependence on the language and style of its Italian musical ancestry. Coincidentally, it was one of Handel's own countrymen, the German expatriate John Christopher Pepusch, who provided the music to Gay's rude lyrics and his jabbing satirical yarn of a hero who was not a Roman general nor an Olympian bard but a swaggering highwayman.

John Christopher Pepusch   John Gay

Pepusch was a composer of some talent; a few of his chamber works still survive. He also was a talented assimilator, and the thrust of *The Beggar's Opera* was deepened by the fact that for many of its best songs, Pepusch had deliberately helped himself to some of Handel's best-known tunes. Thanks to Gay's deliberate vulgarity, these familiar songs became merciless burlesques of themselves.

The results are well-known. *The Beggar's Opera* opened in a small theater in Lincoln's Inn Fields on January 29, 1728. The audience was taken by surprise; but it remained to cheer, and the work was an instant hit. Not only that: so great was its success that it turned the lance of ridicule on Handel himself. Within weeks of the opening of *The Beggar's Opera,* Handel's troupe at the Royal Academy went bankrupt.

Beyond all this, *The Beggar's Opera* initiated a new kind of opera. Instead of the noble lyric artifice of the Italian models—beautiful as the best of them were—here was a musical drama set in the language of its audience. Its action was spoken (and therefore faster-moving) rather than sung as recitative, its music was derived from (or, at least, close to) music the crowd already knew, and its plot was full of comedic or folk influences. *The Beggar's Opera* itself spawned several descendants, many of them using characters from the original plot. The musical style was exported onto the Continent and became the basis for French and German imitations that also employed the vernacular, lightweight plots, and spoken dialogue. Such a work as Mozart's *The Magic Flute* can trace its bloodlines clearly back to this 1728 masterpiece of Pepusch and Gay, as can a masterwork of our own time, *The Threepenny Opera,* in which the German playwright Bertolt Brecht reworked Gay's original libretto and the composer Kurt Weill created an amazingly fluent synthesis of oldish-sounding music and late-1920s jazz.

The Beggar's Opera

Selected Recordings

The Beggar's Opera

Nigel Rogers, Angela Jenkins, Shirley Minty, and Edgar Fleet, with Denis Stevens and the Chorus and Orchestra of the Accademia Monteverdiana *(ABC)*

John Cameron, Elsie Morison, Monica Sinclair, and Owen Brannigan, with Sir Malcolm Sargent and the Pro Arte Ensemble *(Angel-Seraphim)*

There is no such thing as an absolutely "authentic" performance of *The Beggar's Opera*. The evidence at hand indicates that many of its surviving songs were added or dropped on a whim. The two versions noted here are both excellently sung and stylishly conducted, and the choice is between a scholar's careful attempt to reconstruct a conjecture of an authentic performance and a famous and clever total rewrite. Stevens is the scholar, and his elegant and lively performance is a fine blending of scholarship and a lively sense of drama. The Sargent performance is of a famous version created in 1920 by Frederick Austin for a London revival. There is some reharmonizing of tunes and some thickening of the original orchestration; yet it ·is hard to ignore the beauty of the result and a silly waste to go around yelling "sacrilege" at something that Gay and Pepusch themselves, being shrewd men of the theater, would surely have perpetrated, given the means.

Supplementary Recordings

ANON,
   The Play of Daniel
   New York Pro Musica conducted by Noah Greenberg
   (MCA)
MONTEVERDI, Claudio *(1567-1643)*
   The Coronation of Poppea
   Carole Bogard, Charles Bressler, and an ensemble conducted by Alan Curtis *(Cambridge)*
CAVALLI, Pier Francesco *(1602-1676)*
   La Calisto
   Ileana Cotrubas, Janet Baker, and Owen Brannigan, with Raymond Leppard and the Glyndebourne Festival Ensemble *(Argo/Decca)*
PURCELL, Henry *(1659-1695)*
   The Fairy Queen
   Alfred Deller conducting a vocal and instrumental ensemble *(Vanguard)*
HANDEL, George Frideric *(1685-1759)*
   Acis and Galatea
   Jill Gomez, Robert Tear, and Benjamin Luxon, with Neville Marriner and the Academy of St. Martin's in the Fields *(Argo/Decca)*
PERGOLESI, Giovanni Battista *(1710-1736)*
   La Serva Padrona
   Rosanna Carteri and Nicola Rossi-Lemeni, with Carlo Maria Giulini and the Orchestra of La Scala *(Seraphim)*

The twelfth- or thirteenth-century *Play of Daniel* was apparently created by students at the Abbey of Beauvais in France as a way of dramatizing Biblical texts for the edification of congregations. The music was found in manuscript and edited by Rembert Weakland and Noah Greenberg for modern performance. To edit a manuscript from that long ago requires enormous imagination and second-guessing, and there is no question that the modern rhythms and jangling sonorities (played, to be sure, on modern copies of old instruments) is a long way from what the Beauvais students had in mind. But the work is an honorable compromise, and the music itself is irresistibly lively, flavorsome and communicative, musical drama in any sense of the word.

Poppea was the last of Monteverdi's operas, composed and first performed in Venice in 1642, a year before the composer's death. It differs greatly from *L'Orfeo* of twenty-five years earlier. Its divisions into distinct scenes, with recitatives leading to arias, points the way to the kind of opera that would dominate Italian tastes for the next two hundred years. Its plot, involving the Roman Emperor Nero's dalliance with the courtesan Poppea and her accession to power, makes it the first known opera to deal with "human" characters, and the power of Monteverdi's music to illuminate human emotions is something that we can still feel. *Poppea* has been re-edited for "modern" performances by several contemporary conductors, but this version successfully reaches a compromise between scholarship and theater, with the stylish Poppea of Carole Bogard an added advantage.

The prolific Cavalli (over forty known operas) was successful among the next "generation" of Venetian composers. A composer with, quite obviously, a solid understanding of popular taste in a city beset with a craze for opera, Cavalli wrote works that mingle high-minded lyrical strength with interludes of low comedy as embarrassing as that of some of Shakespeare's clowns. *La Calisto* is a superb mingling of both, and even though Raymond Leppard's modern edition is somewhat too lush in both harmony and orchestration, this is another instance where sheer beauty (including that of Janet Baker's singing) outweighs all arguments.

The Fairy Queen is not an opera, nor is it related to the Spenser poem. It is a paraphrase by one Elkanah Settle of *A Midsummer Night's Dream,* produced in London in 1692, for which Purcell provided an extended score of songs, dances, choruses, and orchestral interludes—all of a grand and festive nature. It sounds the opposite side of this remarkable composer's gifts from that of *Dido and Aeneas.* It is fabulously colorful and, for all its prolixity, not a note too long. Similarly, the pastoral, simple nature of Handel's *Acis and Galatea,* composed in 1717—and thus predating his important operas—is an interesting and delectable contrast to the grandeur of his Italianate works. Here is a composer, newly arrived in a strange land, composing in a language he could not yet speak, and doing so with consummate elegance.

Giovanni Pergolesi's dates indicate that he died tragically young. Yet in his 26 years he created a number of choral works of great eloquence and, better yet, the short two-character comic opera *The Maid as Mistress,* using an old-fashioned farce plot about the ambitious serving-girl who dupes an old fool into marriage. The work lasts less than an hour and was originally composed as a short entertainment to go between the acts of a longer, more serious grand opera; yet the easy melodiousness of Pergolesi's music won hearts after the longer work was forgotten, and this tiny work became the progenitor of the Italian farce-comic style which, along with England's *Beggar's Opera,* was to bring about the growth of a new kind of opera, one free of the encrustations of Baroque artificiality.

2.
Opera and the Human Drama

The course of opera in its first 150 years seems to resemble a circle. Its first practitioners, around 1600, proclaimed themselves the saviors of music as the handmaiden of drama. The first operas were, in fact, little more than paraphrases of classic drama declaimed according to the rise and fall of an expressive musical line discreetly supported by a harmonizing bass line. Then came the artifice, the creation of tuneful arias that allowed singers to win the hearts of the crowd, even though the forward motion of the story was often delayed for absurd lengths of time. Early in the eighteenth century came several kinds of artistic reaction against this kind of operatic artifice: Gluck, with his powerful lyric dramas shorn of pandering to the whims of singers and their fans; Pergolesi, with his light-textured, swift, tuneful farces; Gay and Pepusch, with their *Beggar's Opera,* which laughed all serious opera off the London stage for years.

Yet these attempts to "reform" opera did not find universal acceptance. Composers, as well as singers, often had a loyal, sometimes slavish following of ardent defenders. In Paris and Vienna, the faction supporting Gluck did battle through pamphlets and polemic articles in the press with the proponents of Niccolò Piccinni, a successful, Italian-born practitioner of the old style. Similarly, adherents of the comic ("buffo") style of Pergolesi precipitated a "War of the Buffonists" with the supporters of the more monumental operatic style of Scarlatti and Handel.

Of course, no victories were scored; the world of opera was, by 1750, vast enough to accommodate many schools of thought on the subject of what could or could not constitute proper operatic composition. The new comedic style of Pergolesi led to the spirited full-length operatic comedies of Domenico Cimarosa and Giovanni Paisiello, and these works—Cimarosa's *The Secret Marriage* and Paisiello's *The Barber of Seville,* in particular—were given throughout Europe. Meanwhile, the greatest writer of operatic texts in the grand, classic manner, Pietro Antonio Domenico Bonaventura Metastasio, lived to see his texts set to music by almost every composer of his time, including Handel and Mozart. Indeed, some Metastasio texts were used by as many as sixty composers.

The variety of opera created during the latter half of the eighteenth century reflected the variety within the opera-going public. The one constancy, in fact, was that opera remained, in almost every European city that could muster any pretense at culture, the most popular form of public entertainment. The grand houses—London's Haymarket, Milan's Teatro Regio Ducale (later La Scala), the San Carlo at Naples, the Opéra at Paris, and Vienna's Burgtheater—gobbled up new works as fast as composers could furnish them. Moreover, in most cities there were also the smaller houses, producing more modest people's opera; these houses, too, were enormously popular. It was from such a house, run by a poet and actor named Emanuel Schikaneder on the outskirts of Vienna, that Wolfgang Amadeus Mozart's final masterpiece, *The Magic Flute,* emerged.

Some important operatic centers remained the playthings of noble patrons, although their days were numbered after the revolutions that swept Europe and America late in the century. It was at the palace of Esterhaz in Austria-Hungary that Joseph Haydn produced a considerable repertory of opera for Prince Nicholas Joseph Esterhazy's invited guests—not the equal of Haydn's symphonic output, perhaps, but splendid of their kind.

It was the miraculously gifted Mozart, however, who seemed to transfigure virtually every kind of operatic thinking that occupied the public attention in the last decades of the eighteenth century. The best Italian comedy, the best of the old-fashioned, monumental, serious opera, the best of the vernacular German light opera (something of a spinoff from *The Beggar's Opera*) all were among Mozart's contributions to the musical life of his world. There is no question that, in all his music, Mozart thought operatically. In the greatest of his orchestral music, the piano concertos that he wrote as a way of eking out a livelihood in Vienna, the give-and-take between soloist and orchestra or among various instrumental forces within the orchestra seems almost always to hover on the brink of breaking into words. The fact that Mozart could, in these works, write operas without words is but further testimony to the mastery of musical drama that illuminates his operas themselves.

Mozart: The Italian Operas

Wolfgang Amadeus Mozart *(1756–1791)*

Le Nozze di Figaro, *K. 492, opera in four acts; text by Lorenzo da Ponte after the Beaumarchais play* Le Mariage de Figaro. *First performance, Vienna, May 1786*

Don Giovanni, *K. 527, opera in two acts; text by Lorenzo da Ponte. First performance, Prague, October 1787*
Così fan Tutte, *K. 589, opera in two acts; text by Lorenzo da Ponte. First performance, Vienna, January 1790*
La Clemenza di Tito, *K. 621, opera in two acts; text by Caterino Mazzola after the play by Metastasio. First performance, Prague, September 1791*

Wolfgang Amadeus Mozart

In May of 1769, at the palace of the Archbishop of Salzburg, an opera was given by a local prodigy whose fame as a child of exceptional gifts as performer, improviser, and composer had already spread throughout Europe—Wolfgang Amadeus Mozart. Mozart was barely 13 when his first full-length opera, a farce-comedy called *La Finta Semplice* (The Pretended Simpleton), had its first performance. Its score is full of delights, but it would take a great deal of hindsight to set it apart from the hundreds of similar lightweight works of the time—pieces by Cimarosa, Paisiello, and a host of others who have mostly been forgotten. Mozart himself would mine this vein often in his prodigal adolescence and would also dabble at least once in the other popular Italian operatic genre, the majestic, formal, serious opera that still held on, long past its heyday.

In 1781 Mozart's *Idomeneo* was given at Munich. It was a long work in the classic style, but the young man had found enough life in that form to create an opera of genuine originality. *Idomeneo,* which is still often given today (best of all, with copious cuts), was successful enough to convince the 25-year-old composer to take off for the world's major musical capital. From 1781 until his death, a mere decade later, Mozart lived, worked, starved, wenched, drank, and married in Vienna—and, along the way, created what is arguably the greatest music ever written.

For Vienna's grand opera Mozart made a few sporadic stabs, but without much luck: two works from his early Viennese years remained unfinished. However, those were the years (1781–86) of the great late piano concertos, the string quartets dedicated to Haydn, and several symphonies, and in all this music the hand of a master operatic composer could be felt—in the way all his music took on the aspect of a vivid drama. Sometimes, indeed, as in the slow movement of the piano concerto (the Concerto in C major, K. 467) that we know today from its use in the movie *Elvira Madigan,* the drama seems almost too poignant to fit mere mortal words.

Then, in 1786, Mozart fell in with Lorenzo da Ponte, that colorful Italian vagabond, sometime poet, and scoundrel, and there occurred one of the greatest meetings of minds in operatic history. Beaumarchais's *The Marriage of Figaro* was a sequel to his popular farce *The Barber of Seville,* which Paisiello had set to music in 1782 (and which a composer as yet unborn, Gioacchino Rossini, would set to incomparably finer music later on). *Figaro* was more than lightweight farce: it was a wry and cynical onslaught on licentious noblemen who abandon their wives and how their philandering can be thwarted by the wisdom of servants. This was an explosive subject in Europe, which was soon to experience major upheavals during and after the French Revolution. Da Ponte had to omit a great deal of the slashing wit in his operatic text, if only to get his words past the Viennese censors.

Mozart's music restores the essence of the great and meaningful human comedy that da Ponte had had to shorten. Here, for the first time, is opera in its ideal state: music and drama inextricably linked to create an artistic oneness on a higher artistic level than either component could attain. Every character in *The Marriage of Figaro* is invested with an unmistakable personality: the boisterous, slightly goofy Figaro; his pert, wise Susanna (whose lovesong in the last act is so divinely simple that it tells us all that the world ever needs to know about first love); Cherubino, the amorous page, all sighs and flutters; the sardonic but ultimately vulnerable count; and, above all, his countess, saddened as her husband neglects her but still in command of enough wit to abet the plot that brings about the would-be seducer's downfall.

Every separate aria in the opera is a finely wrought portrait of a character and an emotion, but the crowning glory of the work—and, indeed, of all of Mozart's Italian operas—is the ensemble writing. Here Mozart can estab-lish the power of music over time; his many characters can be simultaneously involved with different strands of plot, yet music allows them to sing together, or in rapid succession, as they could not in a play. Listen, for example, to the start of the long finale in the second act. The count believes that the countess has a lover hiding in her closet. He demands the key—in a musical phrase of stark, stentorian tone. She, terrified, refuses, and her phrase is a sort of garrulous, dithering portrait of confusion. Then the closet door opens, revealing that the person inside is only the maid, Susanna. Suddenly, the count's music is spaced out in long, slow notes: he has been rendered very nearly speechless. The countess, on the other hand, is now in control; she and Susanna join in a clear scolding of the now-baffled count.

In all three of the operas composed with da Ponte, Mozart found the ideal artistic force to inspire his incredible and unique fund of dramatic devices.

Le Nozze di Figaro

In the third act of *Figaro,* Susanna and the countess write a letter to trap the count in a rendezvous. The letter itself is a hilarious send-up of inane, sentimental poetry, and Mozart sets it to equally sentimental, almost gooey music in which the two women blend voices in something close to barbershop harmony. In the last of their three operas, *Così fan Tutte,* Mozart and da Ponte were involved with a totally simple-minded, rather absurd plot: two lovers test their sweethearts' fidelity by pretending to go off to war and then returning in disguise to woo them. To make such a plot work, Mozart indulged in a great deal of the same kind of parody of love music as that employed in *Figaro.* The girls sing in rich, sugary harmonies throughout, and later on the boys serenade them in a marvelously overdrawn nocturne. When one of the girls determines to remain true "like a rock" to her departed beloved, Mozart gives her another kind of parody, an almost unsingable spoof of the virtuosic, hysterical aria with which mythological creatures in old-fashioned opera had defended *their* honor.

Figaro remains the most poignant of the operas because of the astounding humanness of its characters. *Così* has become popular only in the last few decades—mostly because its plot had formerly been variously dismissed as immoral or artificial; but nowadays we know that its very artifice, the symmetry of its manipulation of pairs of pairs, makes it a cherishable work. Between these two in time came the most astounding work of all, the "joyous drama" of *Don Giovanni,* the Don Juan of legend who seduces everyone in his path and is sent to his doom when the statue of a man he has murdered, the father of one of his intended victims, comes to his palace and drags him down to the eternal flames of Hell.

Da Ponte drew his libretto from several sources but fashioned a story whose range of contrast—both of character and of mood—is like no opera hitherto created. The Don is a purveyor of evil. The very opening scene, in which the libertine struggles with the hysterical Donna Anna, is confronted by her father, and then duels with and kills the old man, sweeps across the stage almost like a single breath of music: yet Mozart sets this fearsome episode off by a wonderful comic touch, the addled terror of the Don's low-life servant Leporello, who watches from the sidelines and provides an almost continual line of antic counterpoint. Later, the Don tries to seduce the country wench Zerlina. In this well-known seduction duet he sings to her in a folk-music-like idiom that she would recognize.

The moods of *Don Giovanni* change with the rapidity of the Don's rapier thrusts. Three masked figures come to Giovanni's palace, where a party is going on. They converse with Leporello against the strains of the well-known minuet but then come forward and in the most haunting, slow melody invoke Heaven's aid in defeating the villain. Later, several characters think they have cornered Giovanni and are about to kill him. When their quarry is revealed as Leporello, the harmony makes a sudden wrench in order to involve us, the audience, in the experience of this surprise. Finally, the denouement, with the stark, pounding music of the statue interrupting one of Don Giovanni's boisterous feasts, leaves us breathless with the suddenness of dramatic change.

Beethoven, who generally adored Mozart's music, found *Don Giovanni* a work of unbearable immorality. Through the nineteenth century the work was written about, reinterpreted, and often misrepresented. Mozart himself was obliged to add slapstick scenes to appease the frivolous Viennese audiences, who found the work too serious. Today, *Don Giovanni* is often discussed as the greatest of operas, but the range of interpretations continues to prove that it can be all things to all people.

The last of Mozart's Italian operas was written in fits and starts during his last year of life—during the time when he also created his last German masterpiece, *The Magic Flute,* and worked on the Requiem Mass that he knew would be his own. It was, curiously enough, a return to the grand, serious opera that he hadn't attempted since *Idomeneo.* This final score, *La Clemenza di Tito,* was, in fact, based on a play by Metastasio, the best-known of all librettists in the heyday of serious opera.

Mozart's sublime music managed to transfigure and rejuvenate the stiff formalism of the somewhat archaic plot—the Roman emperor Titus, faced with an epidemic of disloyalty among his most trusted supporters, first dooms and then pardons them all. Nevertheless, *Tito* was long overlooked: its first American performance didn't take place until 1952! One of its main problems is that, as with most opera in its genre, many of the male roles were written for the *castrato* voice and therefore must be sung by women today—a situation that creates difficulties in both staging and casting. Nevertheless, as recent performances have shown, the risks are worth taking. *Tito* is, at least, fairly short, and the sublime beauty of its music, along with the richness of the orchestration (in which the clarinet, the most "human" of all instruments as Mozart wrote for it, almost becomes a character in the drama), are just now attracting worldwide attention.

A final note, by the way, about Lorenzo da Ponte. Shortly after collaborating on *Così fan Tutte,* his fortunes took him to London, where he seems to have gotten into bad company. Around 1800 he got to New York, one step ahead of debtor's prison. In New York he taught Italian literature at Columbia University and ran a bookstore. One of his benefactors was the Pastor of St. Luke's, the Reverend Clement Clark Moore, who is best known for some lines that start " 'Twas the night before Christmas...." In 1825 da Ponte turned impresario and sponsored the first American visit of an Italian opera company, whose repertory included *Don Giovanni.* Da Ponte died in New York in 1838, and he rests today in one of that city's municipal cemeteries.

Selected Recordings
Le Nozze di Figaro
    Hilde Gueden, Suzanne Danco, Lisa della Casa,

Cesare Siepi, and Alfred Poell, with Erich Kleiber and the Vienna Philharmonic Orchestra *(London/Decca)*

Mirella Freni, Jessye Norman, Yvonne Minton, Wladimiro Ganzarolli, and Ingvar Wixell, with Colin Davis and the BBC Symphony Orchestra *(Philips)*

Anna Moffo, Elisabeth Schwarzkopf, Christa Ludwig, Eberhard Waechter, and Giuseppe Taddei, with Carlo Maria Giulini and the Philharmonia Orchestra *(Angel/EMI)*

Don Giovanni

Ina Souez, Luise Helletsgruber, Audrey Mildmay, John Brownlee, Salvatore Baccaloni, and Koloman van Pataky, with Fritz Busch and the Glyndebourne Festival Orchestra *(Vox-Turnabout/EMI)*

Margaret Price, Sylvia Sass, Lucia Popp, Bernd Weikl, Gabriel Bacquier, and Stuart Burrows, with Sir Georg Solti and the London Philharmonic Orchestra *(London/Decca)*

Edda Moser, Kiri Te Kanawa, Teresa Berganza, Ruggero Raimondi, José van Dam, and Kenneth Riegel, with Lorin Maazel and the Paris Opera Orchestra *(Columbia/CBS)*

Così fan Tutte

Lisa della Casa, Christa Ludwig, Emmy Loose, Anton Dermota, Erich Kunz, and Paul Schoeffler, with Karl Boehm and the Vienna Philharmonic Orchestra *(Richmond/HMV)*

Pilar Lorengar, Teresa Berganza, Jeanne Berbié, Ryland Davies, Tom Krause, and Gabriel Bacquier, with Sir Georg Solti and the London Philharmonic Orchestra *(London/Decca)*

La Clemenza di Tito

Lucia Popp, Janet Baker, Yvonne Minton, Frederica von Stade, Stuart Burrows, and Robert Lloyd, with Colin Davis and the Royal Opera House Orchestra *(Philips)*

Out of the luxuries of choice that accompany all of Mozart's best-known operas, two things are certain. One is that no single performance of this kaleidoscopic music can ever please everyone, because of the range of validities in the way the music can be made to work. The other is that, whatever glories a cast may display in performing one of these works, the final accounting comes from the conductor.

As one of many proofs, consider the oldest of the many recordings listed here, the 1936 performance of *Don Giovanni* at Britain's Glyndebourne Festival. There, under the conducting of the late Fritz Busch in the years before the Second World War, Mozart's operas were virtually "rescued" from decades of misunderstanding. Busch's incredibly vivid performance of *Don Giovanni* doesn't have a single international star in its cast—although the young Salvatore Baccaloni, here a most elegant Leporello, went on to greater popularity with the Metropolitan Opera company in New York City in very inelegant, hammed-up comic roles. Nevertheless, this recording has remained through the years a beacon light, a challenge to all who would make this opera work. The recording is ancient but, especially in the EMI remastering, remains vivid.

Several other performances of choice represent a more recent great era in the Mozart renaissance. It took hold in Vienna in the decade after the Second World War, when, in quarters that had to be improvised while the bombed-out Opera was being rebuilt, some splendid young singers—among them the radiant soprano Lisa della Casa and the elegant baritone Erich Kunz—worked with Karl Boehm and, above all, the late Erich Kleiber to rekindle the image of Mozart as love-object. And so the Kleiber *Figaro* of 1953, another relic of the past, is very close to unchallengeable.

Among more recent conductors, the sane, clear work of Colin Davis is generally commendable, and his performance of *La Clemenza di Tito* has in its cast virtually the honor roll of American and British mezzo-sopranos, taking on all those parts originally for male altos. And there is Sir Georg Solti, whose dazzling propulsiveness some may find a little racy for Mozart. But *Don Giovanni,* of all operas, can absorb that approach, and the Solti performance has the incredibly powerful Anna of Margaret Price to give it a place of honor. The performance under Lorin Maazel is also spirited and intelligent, and the work of Edda Moser and Kiri Te Kanawa is outstanding. This album was also the basis for Joseph Losey's wretched film of *Don Giovanni;* shorn of that sad association, however, the performance itself holds up quite well.

Mozart: The German Operas

Wolfgang Amadeus Mozart *(1756–1791)*

Die Entführung aus dem Serail *(The Abduction from the Seraglio), K. 384, opera in three acts; text by Gottlieb Stephanie. First performance, Vienna, July 1782*

Die Zauberflöte *(The Magic Flute), K. 620, opera in two acts; text by Emanuel Schikaneder. First performance, Vienna, September 1791*

The success of *The Beggar's Opera* began a movement toward a new kind of opera that had spoken drama and simple, catchy music and was sung in the language of its audience. This trend spread to the Continent soon after the 1728 premiere: in France, and especially in Germany, this new musical drama found ready acceptance with the crowd. In France the new kind of musical drama took the name *opéra-comique;* in Germany, *Singspiel* (or, simply, a play with singing).

In Germany in particular, a specific kind of plot became enormously popular: a maiden is imprisoned by some form of dirty (or, at least, lecherous) older man, and her rescue is effected by her true lover. In accordance with the popular poetry of the time (the lyrics of Goethe, in particular), these plays were usually given a setting in some strange land—most often, Asia or North Africa. This convention played into the public's passion for exotic settings in operas, beginning with Rameau's *Les Indes Galantes* (or even before). In the typical Singspiel plot, there were usually two pairs of lovers—one noble and highborn, and one (usually servants of the noble lovers) boisterous and comic.

Not long after arriving in Vienna, Mozart found himself with an invitation to submit an opera, in German and of lightweight substance, to Vienna's popular Burgtheater, and for the occasion he found just the kind of exotic rescue tale that the crowd demanded. In the *Abduction,* however, he contributed a considerable amount of effort to raise the standards of the work. There are the basic pairs of lovers: the highborn Constanze and her ardent rescuer Belmonte and their comic servants Blondchen and Pedrillo. The stern Pasha, who holds Constanze in durance vile, is entirely a speaking role, but there is an emissary from the side of the villains, the Pasha's servant Osmin, a wonderfully comic *basso profundo* part. All these characters get a fine variety of music. Both Belmonte and Constanze have long and subtle arias that are somewhat more serious than this type of opera usually absorbed; also, at the end of the second act, when the four lovers are first brought together, they meet in a complex quartet whose dramatic counterpoint clearly points ahead to the kind of writing we find in *Figaro.*

The *Abduction* was a huge success. For all the complexity of some of its more serious moments, there are other features with which Mozart clearly was out to win the crowd: the comic arias and duets involving Osmin and, in the orchestra, an assortment of percussion instruments (cymbals, triangle, and the bass drum) that made a braver and louder noise than most operas of the day afforded.

Nine years later Mozart—mortally ill but still able to manage a few good days—again fell in with a Singspiel project—this time for a small house outside the walls of Vienna, where a sometime poet, singer, and actor named Emanuel Schikaneder ran a troupe of comedians. Schikaneder proposed to Mozart another rescue opera in an exotic setting, again with villains, highborn lovers (whose path through danger in this case would be assured by the presence of a Magic Flute), and a pair of comic lovers, grotesque and almost as much bird as human.

From the beginning, Mozart and Schikaneder, members of the same Freemasons' lodge at a time when the society was under official ban from the Austrian emperor, intended to inject a note into their play that would come across as a secret message from the Masons: the significance of the number three and the use of rituals similar to Masonic initiation ceremonies. However, somewhere along the line, the plot seems to have gotten out of control. Midway in the opera's plot, the supposedly evil Sarastro, who has stolen the lovely Pamina from her mother, the Queen of the Night, becomes a wise and benevolent leader, and the pathetic Queen turns villain. If Mozart or Schikaneder noticed the inconsistency, it apparently meant little. In any event, the opera consumed all of Mozart's waning energies: not ten weeks after its opening, the composer was dead.

The Magic Flute is a work impossible to cope with rationally. Its plot line is of an epic silliness, even discounting the shift in direction. How could a composer with Mozart's sublime instinct for drama set the text to music with a straight face? We will never know, but what we do know is enough. Here, in this sovereign score from the waning days of classicism, the romantic ideal of opera seems to take shape on Mozart's stage. Every character in this motley collection has music with uncanny powers of personal depiction: the noble Tamino, whose ardent love songs are answered by the loving but unhappily constrained Pamina; the delicious pseudo-folk melodies of the bird-catcher Papageno and, at the end, his ladylove

Papagena; the hysterical coloratura of the Queen; and the broad and noble lines of the high priest Sarastro—the only music, George Bernard Shaw once wrote, that could be put into the mouth of God without blasphemy.

The orchestral sounds of *The Magic Flute* are themselves extraordinary. Solemn trombones—often sounding "Masonic" chords in groups of three—and lower wind instruments give much of the music a robust, romantic warmth that seems to forecast the way Richard Wagner would later use the orchestra. The remarkable music that accompanies the lovers' trial by fire and water—Tamino's flute resounding against muffled drums and trumpets—takes music farther than any composer had yet taken it. It is all of this—not its hopeless dramatic substance and the doggerel of Schikaneder's silly libretto—that keeps *The Magic Flute* among the sublime experiences in opera.

Selected Recordings

The Abduction from the Seraglio

    Arlene Augér, Reri Grist, Peter Schreier, and Kurt Moll, with Karl Boehm and the Dresden State Opera Orchestra *(Deutsche Grammophon)*

    Ilse Hollweg, Lois Marshall, Leopold Simoneau, and Kurt Böhme, with Sir Thomas Beecham and the Royal Philharmonic Orchestra *(Angel/EMI)*

The Magic Flute

    Tiana Lemnitz, Erna Berger, Helge Roswaenge, Gerhard Hüsch, and Wilhelm Strienz, with Sir Thomas Beecham and the Berlin Philharmonic *(Turnabout/ EMI World Records)*

    Pilar Lorengar, Christina Deutekom, Stuart Burrows, Hermann Prey, and Martti Talvela, with Sir Georg Solti and the Vienna Philharmonic Orchestra *(London/ Decca)*

    Anneliese Rothenberger, Edda Moser, Peter Schreier, Walter Berry, and Kurt Moll, with Wolfgang Sawallisch and the Bavarian State Opera Orchestra *(Angel/EMI)*

Although every one of these recordings includes splendid individual performances, only one is the kind of peerless total performance that Mozart deserves, and that is the ancient (1938) performance of *The Magic Flute* assembled in Berlin under Beecham. At that, the word *total* must be taken warily, because the performance omits all spoken dialogue. Nevertheless, the cast was, in its time, the excelsis of Mozartian performing units, and Beecham's marvelous wit comes through even in the old monaural recording. Try to get the EMI remastering of the original 78s. The set is more expensive than the Turnabout, but the sound is superior.

Beecham is also the dominant element in the second of the two *Abduction* performances, and there is some elegant phrasing by the Canadian tenor Leopold Simoneau. However, the fact remains that a better *Abduction* than either of the two listed is badly needed. As for the other recordings of *The Magic Flute,* the Solti may strike some as hard-driven (and they will probably enjoy the more modest values in the Sawallisch album), but the very sounds Solti elicits—especially the marvelous blend of the Viennese winds in Mozart's ravishing scoring—is worth the price of the album.

It should also be noted that, for operas with considerable spoken dialogue, at least one English version ought to be recorded. Let it be *The Magic Flute* in the most elegant translation made by W. H. Auden and Chester Kallman for a performance on American television—commercial television, at that—during that medium's palmier days.

Fidelio and Freischütz: Early German Opera

Ludwig van Beethoven *(1770–1827)*

Fidelio, *opera in two acts; text by Josef Sonnleithner and Georg Friedrich Treitschke, based on a French text by Jean-Nicolas Bouilly. First performance, Vienna, November 1805; first performance of revised version, Vienna, May 1814*

Carl Maria von Weber *(1786–1826)*

Der Freischütz, *opera in three acts; text by Friedrich Kind. First performance, Berlin, June 1821*

Ludwig van Beethoven

Twelve years after Mozart's death, Emanuel Schikaneder was still writing opera librettos, although none so successful as *The Magic Flute*. He had advanced to the managership of one of Vienna's most popular theaters, the Theater an der Wien (which still flourishes), and in 1803 was engaged in the creation of a fantastic-heroic opera called *Vesta's Fire*, with music by the 33 year-old Ludwig van Beethoven, the unruly reigning genius of Vienna's music. The project came to naught, but from it Beethoven became inflamed with the desire to create an opera.

His eye eventually fell on a French drama in which a heroic and faithful wife, disguised as a youth, takes a menial job at a prison and brings about the rescue of her husband Florestan, who has been unjustly locked up there. The plot accorded with the still-reigning taste for stories involving rescue (as with Mozart's two German operas), but the strong extra element of personal heroism overcoming political tyranny was, for Beethoven, an added enticement. It did not matter at all that this play—called in the original French *Léonore, ou l'amour conjugal*—had already been made into an opera by one Pierre Gaveaux in Paris and that another composer, Ferdinando Paër, was readying a version in Italian. Nobody seems to have been bothered in those days with exclusive story rights: a good operatic text might be set to music dozens of times by as many composers.

Josef Sonnleithner, one of Beethoven's few close friends, translated the French text fairly literally, and Beethoven set it to music with enormous gusto; yet the resultant opera, as first introduced at the Theater an der Wien in 1805, was a total fiasco. One reason may have been circumstantial: Napoleon had led his armies into Vienna that very week, and the audience on opening night was largely made up of French officers, most of whom were not conversant with German and probably not well-disposed to seeing one of their own countrymen's operatic texts reworked by an uncouth Viennese upstart.

Fidelio

However, there are other reasons for the failure of this version. The original play was something of a mish-mash: on the one hand, there is the heroic rescue; on the other, a rather folksy tale wherein the disguised Leonora must fend off the amorous daughter of the chief jailer. The intensity of Beethoven's setting of the dramatic elements of the plot —the incarnation of evil in the villainous tyrant Pizarro, the lambent courage of Leonora, and the extraordinary dramatic music in the climactic quartet, when Leonora sheds her disguise and holds Pizarro at bay with his own pistol—must necessarily clash, almost beyond reconciliation, with the chirpy folksong-like music for the pastoral characters and the homey philosophizing of the kindly old jailer, one of opera's authentic bores.

The failure of this first *Fidelio* was a terrible blow to Beethoven for a time. Then, in 1814, he returned to his opera at the urging of a new friend, G. F. Treitschke, who reworked the libretto drastically. Now the burning spirit of Leonora was given its full range, most of all in a brand-new aria in which she prays for the return of hope and a trio of French horns wreath her thoughts in musical flames. Now the plight of the imprisoned Florestan is given new weight, as in his first aria—in which the vision of his Leonora sends him into momentary frenzy. Now the heroism of the plot is brilliantly highlighted by two huge and contrasting choral episodes: the harrowing chorus of prisoners that ends the first act and the triumphant hymn to wifely virtue that brings down the final curtain.

None of these elements had been in the first *Fidelio*, and they are the best-known glories of its revision. As it stands, *Fidelio* still has problems. Even after his pruning, the new librettist had to leave enough of the folksy side of the plot to give the basic drama some kind of setting; therefore, the transition from pastoral love-making to the cataclysmic true drama must always come as a jolt. In spite of this, the music that follows makes ample amends.

Fidelio has never been out of the world's repertory since its triumphant "rebirth." Moreover, even though its story was French in origin and the plot itself is set in Spain, it was widely hailed in Germany and Austria as a major step in establishing a native repertory of opera that was German not only in language but in feeling. This time—the first two decades of the nineteenth century—was, especially in the German-speaking world, a time of ethnic consciousness, a flame much fanned by the appearance of several collections of folk poetry, both genuine and newly "invented," as it were.

Carl Maria von Weber

The German-born Carl Maria von Weber—whose niece Constanze had been the wife of Mozart—was caught up in this passion for folk expression, and the most notable result was his opera *Der Freischütz,* an instant success after its 1821 premiere in Berlin and a work whose seminal force in establishing German opera was freely acknowledged in years to come by Richard Wagner.

Friedrich Kind's plot draws upon elements central to all German story-telling: the forest with its elements both beneficial and terrifying, the exaltation of the purest of pure maidenhood, and a drama involving huntsmen, merrymakers' drinking songs, and a faltering hero redeemed through love. The music itself throbs with the rhythms of folk song and folk dance—with, of course, some material of more elevated musical structure to depict the passion of the hero, the free-shooter Max, and his beloved Agathe.

But the most remarkable scene in *Der Freischütz* was like nothing ever put into an opera before (although the ritualistic scenes in *The Magic Flute* came close). In order to win the marksmanship contest and claim Agathe's hand, Max has let himself be lured—at midnight, naturally —into the dread Wolf's Glen, deep in the forest. There, guided by the villainous Kaspar, he meets the Black Hunter himself. Max must cast seven magic bullets out of a mixture that includes molten lead, glass from church windows, the eye of an owl, and a great deal of mumbo jumbo. The depictive power of Weber's music—especially the spooky harmonies and the groans and shrieks from the orchestra—brought into the opera house the same magical and haunting "once-upon-a-time" elements that the Grimm Brothers were putting into their startling fairy tales. Not many decades thereafter, Richard Wagner would allow this same spirit to guide his pen in his first successful music drama, *The Flying Dutchman.*

Selected Recordings

Fidelio

Gundula Janowitz, Lucia Popp, René Kollo, Dietrich Fischer-Dieskau, and Hans Sotin, with Leonard Bernstein and the Vienna Philharmonic Orchestra *(Deutsche Grammophon)*

Helge Dernesch, Helen Donath, Jon Vickers, Zoltan Kelemen, and Karl Ridderbusch, with Herbert von Karajan and the Berlin Philharmonic *(Angel/EMI)*

(original 1805 version, erroneously identified here as *Leonore*) Edda Moser, Helen Donath, Richard Cassilly, Theo Adam, and Karl Ridderbusch, with Herbert Blomtedt and the Dresden State Opera Orchestra *(Ara-esque–EMI)*

Der Freischütz

Gundula Janowitz, Edith Mathis, Peter Schreier, Bernd Weikl, and Theo Adam, with Carlos Kleiber and Dresden State Opera Orchestra *(Deutsche Grammophon)*

The 1970 Bernstein recording of *Fidelio,* produced in Vienna for the Beethoven bicentennial, is a remarkable piece of work all around: for the thrust of Bernstein's own conception and for the generally magnificent singing by a cast long identified with this opera. Do not, however, be misled into assuming that later Bernstein performances, with Gwyneth Jones as Leonora, even begin to match this earlier version: the distortion in musical values here could constitute a study in a conductor's changing attitudes that verges on a sociological document. The Karajan–Berlin Philharmonic recording is also excellent—most of all for the plangent, intensely moving delivery by Jon Vickers of Florestan's great second-act aria. The 1805 version, for the reasons noted, cannot stand as anyone's only version of the opera (although the singing and conducting are exceptionally fine); but a comparison of the 1805 and 1814 scores is a fascinating project on its own, and the earlier score does contain some rather pretty—if dramatically irrelevant—music that Beethoven later dropped.

There are versions of *Der Freischütz* available besides the one on the list—including a drastically abridged performance on Deutsche Grammophon that preserves the spine-chilling Kaspar of George Hann—but the performance conducted by the young Carlos Kleiber (whose late father, Erich, conducted the best *Marriage of Figaro* on records) has the ravishing Agathe of Gundula Janowitz and a finely detailed version of the "Wolf's Glen Scene" in which musical and melodramatic values are kept in balance. That's a hard thing to achieve in this strange but lovable score!

Grand Opera In France

Giacomo Meyerbeer *(1791–1864)*
Le Prophète, *opera in four acts; text by Eugène Scribe. First performance, Paris, April 1849*

Hector Berlioz *(1803–1869)*
Les Troyens (The Trojans), *opera in two parts* (The Capture of Troy *and* The Trojans at Carthage), *five acts; text by Berlioz, based on Virgil's* Aeneid. *First performance (Part II only), Paris, November 1863; first performance of both parts (on two evenings), Karlsruhe (Germany), December 1890*

The French operatic taste was first formed as far back as 1670, when the Italian-born Lully established himself at the court of Louis XIV. In a sense, it remained constant thereafter for at least two centuries: a passion for stately drama with a great deal of spectacle, many dance sequences, and subject matter—drawn from history or legend—that was dignified and grand. It is hardly an accident that the particular type of opera out of which Beethoven found inspiration for his *Fidelio,* the "horror and rescue" genre, was also firmly rooted in Paris around 1800. It was also hardly surprising that the leading Parisian proponent of opera was not a Frenchman at all but an alien—once again, an Italian, Luigi Cherubini.

Furthermore, it was yet another alien who preserved the French operatic style against all comers and raised it to heights of popularity to which artistic merit contributed hardly at all. This immigrant was the German-Jewish Jakob Liebmann Beer, who migrated to Paris in 1826 and changed his name to Giacomo Meyerbeer—a peculiar mix of Italian and German, unlike Lulli-Lully's simpler Gallicizing of his Italian name. Falling in with the leaders of French opera—notably the prolific playwright and librettist with the appropriate name of Scribe—Giacomo Meyerbeer began a series of spectacle-operas to which the public flocked in droves.

These Meyerbeer operas were written with juicy roles for the leading singers of the day, but the elements that drew the crowds were the massive scenes involving chorus, fancy stage effects, and dance. In this sense, Meyerbeer's operas can really be taken as the last waning of the classic line that had begun a century before in the lyric tragedies of Rameau—now, however, somewhat magnified in scope and also, alas, somewhat coarsened.

Nevertheless, there are a couple of almost-masterpieces of a kind among these works: *Les Huguenots* (1836), with its re-enactment on stage of the tragic massacre of the Huguenots in Paris in 1572 (to which, of course, a fanciful love story was appended), and *Le Prophète,* which is set at the time of the Anabaptist revolt in Leyden in 1535. In the latter work, in particular, there is a genuine power in some of the scenes and a purity in the writing for the leading female role—that of Fides, mother of the self-proclaimed prophet John of Leyden—that evoke the classic elegance of great French theater. There is also, for reasons difficult to explain within the scope of one slim volume, an extended ballet sequence in which the dancers are supposed to be on ice skates. This sequence, which is often done by ballet companies as *Les Patineurs,* is, along with the "Coronation March" from this same opera, the only music by Meyerbeer that has remained popular.

Les Troyens

In his time, Meyerbeer's operas were constantly given, while the one work in the realm of Parisian grand opera that merits attention for its music lay unperformed in its entirety until twenty years after its composer's death. That was the gigantic setting by Hector Berlioz of two episodes from the *Aeneid* of Virgil: the fall of Troy as its people, deaf to the warnings of Cassandra, accept the gift of the Wooden Horse from the presumably departing Greeks; and the arrival of the fleeing Trojans at the Carthaginian court of

Queen Dido, the romance between Dido and the Trojan leader Aeneas, and the tragic end as Aeneas abandons Dido and she takes her own life. Henry Purcell had set the story of Dido and Aeneas in a far shorter, simpler opera nearly two centuries before Berlioz, and the two works make for a fascinating comparison.

The splendor of *The Trojans* has really been assessed only in our lifetime, thanks to productions of the work in London, Boston, and New York—the first performances ever to use the composer's score without cuts. The daring of the work, the dark, menacing orchestral outcries in the first part and the lush, seamless melodies that underline the love music later on—not to mention the opera's most familiar episode, the music for orchestra and chorus depicting a royal hunting party and the storm that overtakes the hunters—set Hector Berlioz apart from the operatic scriveners of his native Paris as an incomparably more original creator.

Selected Recordings

Le Prophète
    Renata Scotto, Marilyn Horne, James McCracken, and Jerome Hines, with Henry Lewis and the Ambrosian Chorus and Royal Philharmonic Orchestra *(Columbia/ CBS)*

Les Troyens
    Berit Lindholm, Josephine Veasey, Jon Vickers, Peter Glossop, and Roger Soyer, with Colin Davis and the Royal Opera House Chorus and Orchestra *(Philips)*
    (Dido's Lament only) Janet Baker, with Alexander Gibson and the London Symphony Orchestra *(Angel/ EMI)*

It is not likely that either of these operas will receive multiple recordings and, in the case of the complete *Les Troyens* under Colin Davis, such a duplication would be foolhardy, so remarkable is this one achievement. Davis's command of the range of color in Berlioz's scoring is a remarkable case of total artistic empathy, and it has established him as the pre-eminent exponent of this strange composer's music. (There are also Davis recordings of the other two Berlioz operas, the ravishing *Béatrice et Bénédict*—its text drawn from Shakespeare's *Much Ado About Nothing*—and *Benvenuto Cellini,* a romance fashioned around the famous Florentine.) The cast in this performance of *Les Troyens* is the one that participated in the 1969

Covent Garden (London) production, the first ever to present the score, uncut and unchanged, as Berlioz had created it over a century before.

The recording of *Le Prophète* also stems from a revival, this time, at the Metropolitan Opera House (New York) in 1975. If the spectacular virtues of the Berlioz album are not duplicated here, this is at least an intelligent assembling of much of the essence of Meyerbeer's oddly affecting score. The best element—in this performance as in the opera itself—is the deeply moving singing of the role of the mother, Fides. It was one of Marilyn Horne's great moments.

Supplementary Recordings

HAYDN, Joseph *(1732–1809)*
Il Mondo della Luna
Arleen Augér, Edith Mathis, and Frederica von Stade, with Antal Dorati and the Lausanne Chamber Orchestra *(Philips)*

PAËR, Ferdinando *(1777–1839)*
Leonora
Ursula Koszut, Edita Gruberova, Siegfried Jerusalem, and Giorgio Tadeo, with Peter Maag and the Bavarian Symphony Orchestra *(London/Decca)*

NICOLAI, Otto *(1810–1849)*
The Merry Wives of Windsor
Edith Mathis, Helen Donath, Peter Schreier, Bernd Weikl, and Kurt Moll, with Bernhard Klee conducting the Berlin State Opera Orchestra *(Deutsche Grammophon)*

HALÉVY, Jacques-François *(1799–1862)*
La Juive (selections)
Martina Arroyo, Anna Moffo, Richard Tucker, and Bonaldo Giaiotti, with Antonio de Almeida and the New Philharmonia Orchestra *(RCA)*

SCHUBERT, Franz *(1797–1828)*
Alfonso und Estrella
Edith Mathis, Peter Schreier, Dietrich Fischer-Dieskau, and Hermann Prey, with Otmar Suitner and the Berlin State Opera Orchestra *(Angel/EMI)*

During his long employment at the Esterhazy Palace, Haydn was occasionally called upon to create operas for the entertainment of the prince's noble guests, although it cannot be said that his achievements in this field had the progressive quality, the devil-may-care sense of adventure, that we can find in his quartets and symphonies. Yet this farce-comedy of 1777, in which a foolish old man is duped into believing that he has been transported to the moon, is full of moonstruck enchantment.

The interest in Paër's *Leonora* is primarily the fact that this is another setting of the libretto that Beethoven used for *Fidelio;* yet this score by a popular Italian craftsman of the time has genuine merits of its own. It doesn't have the grandeur of Beethoven's version, but what other opera does? It even lacks a chorus; yet the music for the two principal characters, Leonora and "Florestano," indicates that Paër had some insight into the strength of these characters.

Throughout his life Schubert struggled with the problem of opera, but the Fortune that dumped an endless stream of song texts into his lap stopped short of operatic generosity. Schubert left the world half a dozen full-length serious operas, plus several one-act works. All of them are full of enchanting music, but they could not conceivably hold the stage. The hopelessly complex plot of *Alfonso und Estrella,* in which the brave hero and loving heroine are united thanks to a magic charm long believed missing, contains music of such radiant beauty that the only thing to do is to discard the libretto and listen.

Otto Nicolai, a German composer prolific despite his relatively brief life, is remembered today entirely for his delightful setting of Shakespeare's comedy. His music has some of Weber's folklike quality, and the final scene, wherein the errant Falstaff is "tamed" at midnight in Windsor Forest, is cloaked in delicious fairy music that could pass for a missing page or two out of Felix Mendelssohn's book.

Jacques-François Halévy was a successful creator of over forty operas in the grand Parisian manner. Today only *La Juive* is heard, and that largely because of its particular ethnic appeal. Here the operatically requisite oppressed choral groups, rather than being Meyerbeer's Huguenots or Anabaptists, are Jewish. The Passover scene could, in fact, be mistaken for a Masonic or Boy Scout ceremony if it had other words, but the music has a certain bland attractiveness and, of course, an undeniable appeal for its ethnic uniqueness.

3.
Opera as Romantic Entertainment

What makes an opera work—on a stage before a packed house, or even on a recording, with the staging merely in our minds? There is no pat formula: so far in this more-or-less historical survey we have encountered operas of unchallenged stature whose musical qualities overcome inadequacies of plot (for example, Mozart's *The Magic Flute*), along with others whose "stage presence" overcomes musical problems (Meyerbeer's *Le Prophète,* to name just one).

There are qualities in a successful opera that defy easy definition. We can think of one of these qualities as a vague "theatrical sense," in which both music and drama participate. Without our knowing a thing about what is to come in the ensuing opera, the very opening chords of Mozart's *Don Giovanni* turn any space—an opera house, or our own record-listening room—into a theater. Another, slightly different quality might be called a "histrionic sense." We come face-to-face with this element when, in the midst of some absurd or peculiar kind of impenetrable musical and dramatic nonsense, there is a sudden confluence of music, drama, and performance that puts everything into context and reminds us once again that opera is an art form unto itself, drawing its strength from its own exotic irrationality.

Such a moment, for example, occurs in the first-act finale of Gioacchino Rossini's *Barber of Seville.* The situation is stock farce. Don Bartolo, a foolish old man, wants to marry the lovely young Rosina. She is also being wooed, with greater success, by a handsome stranger, Lindoro (who is really the Count Almaviva in disguise), and the barber Figaro is helping this romance along. The first-act finale is a whirl of action whose two purposes are first, to get Lindoro into Bartolo's house and thus close to Rosina and second, to drive Bartolo crazy in the process.

All is proceeding according to plan: Lindoro (who is now further disguised as a drunken soldier) has created an uproar that has brought a whole squad of police onto a stage already full of people; the music gets faster and louder to underscore the turmoil. But then composer and librettist hit upon a purely histrionic device to turn the screw even further: one soldier inadvertently drops his musket, and the noise becomes, for poor Bartolo, the last straw. He is rendered catatonic—"cold and motionless, like a statue," the ensemble sings. The music also gears down suddenly from enormous bustle to near-immobility, although it maintains its momentum and hilarity.

It is this kind of sheer theatrical and histrionic inventiveness that conspires to keep the great works of Romantic opera fresh and vivid, against all reasonable arguments. To be sure, the plotting is full of dramatic absurdity and the hoariest of devices. Certainly, the artistic momentum can be dispensed with for long moments to appease the ego of a star soprano or tenor. Of course, there are times when the music itself seems like a mere saccharine coating to the dramatic situation. Still, there is a genuine theatricality in the best of this music that can be taken only on its own terms, and when there are singers on hand to realize its full extent, the element of pure histrionic bedazzlement outweighs any argument. Seeing the scene from *The Barber of Seville* staged by a director who also understands the marvelous wit of the music at that point; hearing the divine soprano Maria Callas, her voice aflame from Bellini's music, confront her faithless lover at the end of *Norma;* sharing the heartbreak of the clown Canio, who must put on the whiteface of his profession (in Leoncavallo's *I Pagliacci*) and laugh, although his wife's infidelity has raddled his brain—these were the experiences that kept opera foremost in the affections of audiences throughout the Western world from the time of Beethoven right into our own century and continue to fascinate and thrill us today.

Opera's spread was truly worldwide in the nineteenth century, yet its heart remained in Italy. The greatest Italian composers enjoyed lustrous fame at home but added other nations to their conquered territory. Rossini settled in Paris and wrote in and for that city his last great operas. Later, Gaetano Donizetti, Vincenzo Bellini, and Giuseppe Verdi were called upon to create works for the Paris Opéra, often in preference to perfectly capable native French composers. Verdi's fame and activities spread even farther. He created *La Forza del Destino* in 1862 on commission from the Imperial Opera at St. Petersburg; nine years later, his *Aida* was first mounted at the Cairo Opera House, commissioned by the Egyptian government to celebrate the opening of the Suez Canal. Virtually every Italian opera that achieved fame at home was soon able to repeat its triumphs elsewhere. Bellini's *La Sonnambula,* to choose an example at random, had its Milan premiere in March of 1831; by July it had been produced in London by the resident company at Her Majesty's Theatre in Haymarket. Four years later it took New York City by storm, in the hands of one of several Italian companies that had, by the 1830s, set roots down in America—a land, needless to add, which was to prove operatically fertile.

Of course, not all Romantic opera was Italian. The currents in Germany—the passionate rediscovery and/or invention of an indigenous folklore—that flowed through Weber and his *Freischütz* would produce, in the person and works of Richard Wagner, a genuine cultural revolution, a way of operatic life that affected both artistic and social styles. Later in the nineteenth century, as a concomitant of an overall stirring in smaller countries toward the assertion of their separate nationalities, opera became an important medium for establishing and reflecting these territorial consciences. Whether or not the Romantic composer of any country chose whole-hearted acceptance of, or the belligerent need to be different from, the body of Italian lyric drama of the Romantic era, the teeming, soaring, sometimes silly, often thrilling operatic language of Italy continued to dominate the opera houses of the world.

Bel Canto

Gioacchino Rossini *(1792-1867)*
Il Barbiere di Siviglia, *opera in two acts; text by Cesare Sterbini, based on Beaumarchais's* Le Barbier de Seville. *First performance, Rome, February 1816*
Guillaume Tell, *opera in four acts; text by Etienne de Jouy and Hippolyte Bis, based on Schiller's play. First performance, Paris, August 1829*

Gaetano Donizetti *(1797-1848)*
Lucia di Lammermoor, *opera in three acts; text by Salvatore Cammarano, based on Sir Walter Scott's* The Bride of Lammermoor. *First performance, Naples, September 1835*
Don Pasquale, *opera in three acts; text by Giovanni Ruffini. First performance, Paris, January 1843*

Vincenzo Bellini *(1801-1835)*
Norma, *opera in two acts; text by Felice Romani. First performance, Milan, December 1831*

Gioacchino Rossini

The term *bel canto* merely means "beautiful singing," and this means, of course, that any opera you can easily name— certainly, any Italian opera— could rank as bel canto. Yet the term has a specific meaning.

As Italy's opera houses grew in size and number early in the nineteenth century, as the fame of its composers spread throughout Europe and across the Atlantic, the whole institution of opera once again became more star-ridden, more dominated by the drive to stage a dazzling show for the largest possible audience, so that the great singers of the era became the be-all and end-all of opera. Complain as composers often did at the way that their simple, elegant, expressive melodies were distorted by all kinds of vocal frills improvised by the singers, the singers had the last word, and the composers knew it.

The music created for the divas of the day and their *divos* (if the word doesn't exist, it should) was designed, first and foremost, to sound sublime as sung by the highest-paid sets of vocal apparatus of the day. The bel canto line can be many things: the self-contained, powerful vocal line of Norma's "Casta diva" in Bellini's masterpiece or the exquisite and fragile "Quando rapita" for Lucia of Lammermoor—a tune which on its reprise can bear the load of an infinity of added ornamentation.

The great and versatile Rossini led the way. He was barely out of his teens when his first comic operas delighted audiences in Venice and Milan; and in 1813 *Tancredi,* his first attempt at grand opera, was another instant success. Throughout his life, Rossini mined both operatic veins with enormous skill.

In comic opera he invented—or at least perfected—a vocabulary of ingenious and witty effects, and his most popular comedy, *The Barber of Seville,* contains most of them. Rossini's comic characters are always granted at least one "patter" song apiece, something full of incredibly difficult tongue-twisting. Figaro's famous "Largo al factotum," which marks his first entrance in *The Barber,* is such a work; later on, foolish old Bartolo furiously lectures the flirtatious Rosina—again in marvelously fleet vocal pattering. Then there is the Rossinian crescendo, a gradual buildup of sound and momentum with both musical and dramatic fascination. In the overture to *The Barber,* as in almost all the Rossini overtures, there is a justly famed crescendo, and the opera itself contains other marvelous specimens. One comes late in the first act, when the old busybody, Don Basilio, tells Bartolo about the wonders of slander as a way of besting one's enemies: the lecture starts as a whisper, and erupts as a "blast of cannons."

The Barber belongs among the world's great operatic comedies. As with Mozart, Rossini at his best had the insight to adjust and balance his work so that every moment brought its own surprise. There are moments of poignant "humanness" here, as there are in Mozart's *Marriage of Figaro.* The Rosina is not merely a pert and saucy soubrette; she has moments of genuine tenderness. Figaro, too—conniving one moment, taking time the next to pat himself on the back for his cleverness—is depicted as a flesh-and-blood creature. *The Barber* is Rossini's best-known comic opera, probably because of the excellence of its libretto and the immense popular appeal of its best-known arias. But there are others of high qualilty: *Cenerentola,* a delightful spoof of the Cinderella story, and *The Italian Maid in Algiers,* a fine send-up of the old rescue-from-the-harem yarn with a twist—this time, the hero's girlfriend arrives in time to rescue *him.*

After Rossini the Italianate comic opera flourished in the hands of his prolific successor Gaetano Donizetti, although it is worth noting that the most elegant of his comedies, *Don Pasquale,* was written on commission from the Théâtre-Italien in Paris. *Pasquale* is a beautifully formed descendant of *The Barber:* once again, a foolish old man tries to wed a girl both too young and too smart for him; once again, he is outwitted by the machinations of a wily baritone and the girl's truelove—who is, need one ask, the tenor. The exquisite refinement that Rossini brought to Italian comedy continues here: there is not only the fund of bubbling, genuinely comic music (coming to its climax in a patter duet in the last act that invariably stops the show); there is also a great deal that is pure ravishment—the poignant lament of the unhappy swain being one sublime moment.

To Rossini and Donizetti both, however, the writing of successful operatic comedy was only one side of their operatic output. From Rossini, too, came a flood of epic musical dramas, somewhat akin to the elevated, statuesque serious opera of the eighteenth century but redeemed by Rossini's own gift for passionate, poignant melody of great sweep. Such a work as *Semiramide,* with its plot based on the classic drama of Voltaire, is revived whenever a soprano and mezzo can be found to cope with its vocal terrors. It is ostensibly an operatic throwback to the time of artifice, but it is made livelier than its models by Rossini's own vivid melodic imagination and his colorful use of his orchestra.

Rossini's last opera, a telling of the legend of *William Tell,* was created in Paris and draws for its model upon both the classical lyric drama and the prevailing Parisian passion for great choral displays, empty-headed grandeur and interminable dance sequences. The plot is the familiar one, part legend and part history: Tell defying the Austrian tyrant Gessler who rules his Swiss village, Gessler forcing Tell to shoot an apple from his son's head, the uprising of the Swiss peasants that finally unseats the tyrant. To this basic story Rossini's libretto adds the requisite love interest (Tell's daughter and a local patriot) and, it goes without saying, the chances for great choral numbers occur frequently. *Guillaume Tell* is a long opera and enormously difficult to produce; yet, coming just a year or two before the start of Meyerbeer's Paris career, it stands as the cornerstone of French grand opera—a genre whose greatest (and only native-born) practitioner, Hector Berlioz, lived for most of his career with his operatic talents ignored.

Donizetti, too, tried his hand at the grand, somewhat static historical drama, and during his lifetime he created several of exceptional strength and originality. The most notable are three operas (written separately; not in any way as a cycle) using characters from British history of the Tudor era: *Anna Bolena* (about the rise and downfall of Anne Boleyn); *Maria Stuarda* (from Schiller's play about the last days of Mary of Scotland); and *Roberto Devereux* (about the disintegration of the romance between Elizabeth I and the Earl of Essex). None of these is the least bit "British" in character (*Devereux* does use "God Save the King" in its overture, despite the fact that the tune was written 150 years after Elizabeth's time). They are, however, full of powerful, thoroughly "Italianate" bel canto melody, and the revival of all three operas, spurred by the interest in this musical style shown by the enterprising sopranos Maria Callas, Beverly Sills, and Joan Sutherland, has brought about a general upgrading of Donizetti's place in the operatic spectrum.

Gaetano Donizetti

Donizetti's major contribution was the development of a new kind of Italian Romantic opera, a more intimate kind of tragedy. In such a work as *Lucia di Lammermoor,* there is a nicely managed sense of melancholy, an emotion that we haven't often met before in opera (except, perhaps, in some of the Countess's music in Mozart's *The Marriage of Figaro*). But Lucy is a melancholy figure; she loves Edgar but is forced by family loyalties to marry someone else and this, of course, triggers the magnificent confrontation (wronged lover arriving at the moment of signing of marriage contract to the Other Guy) in the famous sextet. In this conflict between love and duty, Lucy of Lammermoor is the direct ancestor of very nearly every Verdi heroine, and Donizetti portrays her magnificently. Even her big show-off piece, the famous "Mad Scene," is along with a time of great vocal fireworks, a most morose reminiscence of the music that Lucy and her Edgar had sung in happy times.

Lucia di Lammermoor

In his thirty-four years, Vincenzo Bellini composed relatively few operas—relative, that is, to the mercurially prolific Donizetti and Rossini. Comic opera appealed to Bellini not at all; the closest he came was in the quiet pastoral charm of *La Sonnambula,* a sweet if somewhat spineless piece about a lady whose presence in the wrong man's bedchamber turns out to be merely a case of sleepwalking.

Norma

But Bellini's *Norma* towers above all his other work and represents in a real sense the culmination of "pure" bel canto. The story is a reversion to old-fashioned epic drama: the Druid priestess, after years of carrying on an illicit love affair with a Roman soldier, falls melodically to pieces when he takes up with another. The story is grandly told; there are fine choruses as the Druids hurl defiances against the occupying Roman forces; everything happens through melody—ravishing, long-breathed melodic arches that merely float on the simplest orchestral support. *Norma* is perfect of its kind, and the final ensemble, as the heroine and her repentant lover walk together to death amid the flames of retribution, can in proper performance cause whole audiences to suspend breathing.

The young Verdi tried his hand at this kind of opera, and Donizetti and Bellini wrote for some time after *Norma*—usually to great acclaim. Nevertheless, this one early masterpiece of Bellini, written only four years after Beethoven's death, embodies the spirit of Italian bel canto as no other score could or did.

Selected Recordings

Il Barbiere di Siviglia

Teresa Berganza, Ugo Benelli, Manuel Ausensi, and Fernando Corena, with Claudio Abbado and the London Symphony Orchestra *(Deutsche Grammophon)*

Maria Callas, Luigi Alva, Tito Gobbi, and Fritz Ollendorf, with Alceo Galliera and Philharmonia Orchestra *(Angel/EMI)*

Beverly Sills, Nicolai Gedda, Sherrill Milnes, and Renato Capecchi, with James Levine and the London Symphony Orchestra *(Angel/EMI)*

Guillaume Tell

Montserrat Caballé, Nicolai Gedda, Gabriel Bacquier, and Gwynne Howell, with Lamberto Gardelli and the Philharmonia Orchestra *(Angel/EMI)*

Lucia di Lammermoor

Maria Callas, Giuseppe di Stefano, and Tito Gobbi,

with Tullio Serafin and the Ensemble of the 1953 Maggio Musicale *(Angel/EMI)*

Maria Callas, Giuseppe di Stefano, and Rolando Panerai, with Herbert von Karajan and the Ensemble of La Scala *(Turnabout/Cetra)*

Joan Sutherland, Luciano Pavarotti, and Sherrill Milnes, with Richard Bonynge and the Royal Opera House Ensemble *(London/Decca)*

Don Pasquale

Adalaide Saraceni, Tito Schipa, Ernesto Badini, and Afro Poli, with Carlo Sabajno and the Ensemble of La Scala *(Seraphim)*

Beverly Sills, Alfredo Kraus, Alan Titus, and Donald Gramm, with Sarah Caldwell conducting the London Symphony Orchestra *(Angel)*

Norma

Maria Callas, Ebe Stignani, Mario Filippeschi, and Nicola Rossi-Lemeni, with Tullio Serafin and the Ensemble of La Scala *(Angel/EMI)*

Montserrat Caballé, Fiorenza Cossotto, Placido Domingo, and Ruggero Raimondi, with Carlo Cillario and the London Philharmonic Orchestra *(RCA)*

If the name of Maria Callas dominates this list, it is because she, of all the accomplished participants in the recent bel canto revival, could manage not only the vocal difficulties of this sublime music, but also its dramatic implications. In truth, there are moments when the Callas voice must be taken on faith, but careful listening will lead you to suspect every time that the forced or pinched note came about as the result of a dramatic impulse stronger than musical considerations. Callas made two recordings each of *Lucia* and *Norma,* of which the earlier in each case is preferable—again, not merely for the voice, but even more for dramatic considerations. By the same token, the *Lucia* with Karajan (which is not a commercial recorded performance at all but a "pirate" of a 1955 live performance now on a commercial release) is even more overpowering dramatically—probably because Callas is there on a stage, communicating to a live audience. For all the faintness of its sound, this is an indispensable recording. Among current singers, only the sumptuous if stately Caballé style challenges the great Callas. The Sills-Levine *Barber* and the Sutherland-Pavarotti *Lucia* are prettily sung and have the advantage of including a great deal of music that is often lopped off in performance—well over a half-hour's worth in the case of *Lucia.*

Finally, a genuine treasure from the past: the wonderful old *Don Pasquale* in which the velvety, light tenor of Tito Schipa is the lovesick Ernesto to the life and in which those great comic singers Badini and Poli have so much fun with their great patter duet that you cannot resist playing it twice. The Sills-Caldwell performance of *Don Pasquale* is, again, very good, but it is outclassed by this once-in-a-lifetime recording, which has been miraculously restored to brimming life.

Verdi: The Rise to Mastery

Giuseppe Verdi *(1813–1901)*

Nabucco, *opera in four acts; text by Temistocle Solera. First performance, Milan, March 1842*
Ernani, *opera in four acts; text by Francesco Maria Piave after Victor Hugo's* Hernani. *First performance, Venice, March 1844*
Rigoletto, *opera in three acts; text by Francesco Maria Piave after Hugo's* Le Roi s'amuse. *First performance, Venice, March 1851*
Il Trovatore, *opera in four acts; text by Salvatore Cammarano. First performance, Rome, January 1853*
La Traviata, *opera in three acts; text by Francesco Maria Piave after Alexandre Dumas's* La Dame aux camélias. *First performance, Venice, March 1853*

Giuseppe Verdi

Much has been made of Verdi's humble origins as the son of peasants, with little access to music beyond what he himself was taught by the village organist, his failed attempt to enter the conservatory at Milan, and the years back in his home town as local bandmaster. It is easy to throw all this back at Verdi, as a rationale for the thread of vulgarity on which his early operas hung: the red-hot brass-band sonorities, the larger-than-life vocal lines. It is always easy for a musical scholar to sniff at anything too easy of access.

Whatever of all this may be applicable to the operas of Verdi's early years, it can hardly be reckoned a sin. He worked hard at a couple of operas during his first years in Milan. These works—one a morose drama, the other a failed attempt to revive Donizettian comedy—are perfectly good scribbling by a young man, newly arrived in town, hearing Bellini and Donizetti for the first time and, with a young man's zeal, thinking he could do better. Later on, he would do just that.

Verdi's third opera was his first success, and it left no doubt that the successor to the first generation of bel canto composers had come onto the scene. *Nabucco* was a grand farrago of an opera, clearly descended from *Norma* in its easy power of mingling high-flown sentimental spectacle (in this case, the plight of the Hebrews in Babylonian captivity) with an equally absurd love-plot involving—as in *Norma*—a passion that crosses enemy lines. But something else was also on Verdi's mind at the time: his personal sorrow at the plight of Italy under the yoke of Austria. With the sheer power of his music to inflame audiences through its enormous attractiveness, Verdi turned *Nabucco* into a political pamphlet, a secret message to his countrymen. He became both a musical and a national hero.

As success overtook Verdi, he turned out operas in a steady flow. Some continued to incorporate secret political messages, but others merely demonstrated a growing fascination for and mastery over the striding accents of Romantic drama. Verdi found kinship in the extravagant pageantry of Schiller and Hugo and struggled with the enigma of Shakespeare, whom he came to master only late in life. One of his great early successes was his setting of Hugo's *Hernani*. Its plot was, for Verdi, a godsend—a brigand who is an exiled nobleman in disguise, a covey of suitors for the same maidenly hand, and scenes of choral splendor, of forgiveness granted, of revenge exacted. It also was a long step forward for Verdi in his constant quest for dramatic consistency. *Ernani* is dazzlingly written for voices, but there is here and there a suspicion that the showiest of arias actually has something to do with the play itself.

Between 1851 and 1853 came the three operas that established Verdi once and for all as the supreme master of Italian opera: three works totally dissimilar, except in the level of their musical quality. *Rigoletto* was the first, and we may still be astounded at the range of sheer human depiction that Verdi lavished on the title role: the tragic hunchbacked jester, who is duped into conniving in first the rape and then the murder of his own daughter. Not a note of this powerful, terse score goes to waste. Every character is believable: the girlish Gilda, her innocent chirping later shading to accents of melancholy, then of sorrow; the licentious Duke and his catchy love ditties; Rigoletto and his outcries of pain. The orchestra, too, participates as an element in the drama: the menacing growls that usher in the paid assassin, Sparafucile; the flicks from the piccolo and the offstage wordless chorus to bring on lightning and wind in the final storm scene.

Most of all, *Rigoletto* steers the course of popular Italian opera toward the premise that Mozart had first suggested nearly a century before: the way in which music can create its own artificial time and allow a multiplicity of action to occur simultaneously. The last-act quartet from *Rigoletto* is so famous in itself that it's easy to overlook the built-in quotient of dramatic genius: four voices blended in music in such a way that each individuality is preserved.

Throughout his career, Verdi made extraordinary, varied use of the many ways that a musical stage could be psychologically divided against itself, which is what actually happens in the *Rigoletto* quartet. *Il Trovatore,* which followed *Rigoletto* into worldwide acclaim, is in some ways a return to the more extroverted spectacle-opera of Verdi's youth, but there is a new sureness in the music that sets it apart, and there is one marvelous scene which again shows this new control over dramatic counterpoint.

In this scene Leonora, the heroine, is about to enter a convent, because she believes that Manrico, her lover, has been killed by his rival, the dastardly Count di Luna. (The plot of *Il Trovatore* is of such a Byzantine complexity that it is often taken as a parody of its own genre; yet it becomes truly parodied, and even more devastatingly, in several of Gilbert and Sullivan's operettas.) Before she arrives, di Luna and his men arrive to head her off. The men deploy around the convent with the sort of muttering, skulking chorus that Verdi had to get somewhere into nearly all his operas. The count himself is at center stage, barking out orders. Then, off inside the convent, a choir of nuns is heard. It is a moment of sheer high nonsense— this stage divided into three dramatic and musical levels— but nobody who hears it remains unmoved. For all its dramatic improbabilities, *Trovatore* is redeemed time and again by the sheer exuberant vibrance of its melodies.

As if to set matters straight, however, Verdi was simultaneously at work on the opera that is the most dramatically realistic and emotionally effective of all his output: his setting of Alexandre Dumas's *La Dame aux camélias* (often known simply as *Camille*). The play was, for its time, a major innovation: a drama set in its own time, one in which a courtesan breaks hearts and still earns our sympathy. Whatever success Dumas may have had with the crowd, it is through Verdi's music in *La Traviata* (The Courtesan) that the measure of the play can be taken. If there is a perfect romantic opera, let this be it.

Again in scenes of remarkable terseness, the full range of operatic devices is used to establish stunning dramatic contrasts: the physical fragility of Violetta against the social frivolity in the opening scene; the frenzied indecision that sweeps through her at the first curtain, when she balances true love against the pleasure-filled, dissipated life that she has been leading; and, above all, the overwhelming emotional power of her long scene with Germont, the father of her lover, that takes up most of the next scene. Here the music flows with the naturalness of human emotion, even of human speech. The traditional separation between recitative and the formally constructed aria has begun to break down. That process of dissolution continued in the later operas of Verdi.

Selected Recordings

Nabucco
> Elena Suliotis, Dora Carral, Bruno Prevedi, Tito Gobbi, and Carlo Cava, with Lamberto Gardelli and the Vienna State Opera Chorus and Orchestra *(London/Decca)*

Ernani
> Leontyne Price, Carlo Bergonzi, Mario Sereni, and Ezio Flagello, with Thomas Schippers and the RCA Italiana Chorus and Orchestra *(RCA)*

Rigoletto
> Maria Callas, Giuseppe di Stefano, and Tito Gobbi, with Tullio Serafin and the Ensemble of La Scala *(Angel/EMI)*
> Renata Scotto, Carlo Bergonzi, and Dietrich Fischer-Dieskau, with Rafael Kubelik and the Ensemble of La Scala *(Deutsche Grammophon)*

Il Trovatore
> Leontyne Price, Fiorenza Cossotto, Placido Domingo, and Sherrill Milnes, with Zubin Mehta and the New Philharmonia Orchestra *(RCA)*

Zinka Milanov, Fedora Barbieri, Jussi Bjoerling, and Leonard Warren, with Renato Cellini and the RCA Chorus and Orchestra *(EMI)*

La Traviata

Victoria de los Angeles, Carlo del Monte, and Mario Sereni, with Tullio Serafin and the Rome Opera *(Angel/EMI)*

Ileana Cotrubas, Placido Domingo, and Sherrill Milnes, with Carlos Kleiber and the Bavarian State Opera *(Deutsche Grammophon)*

Beverly Sills, Nicolai Gedda, and Rolando Panerai, with Aldo Ceccato and Royal Philharmonic Orchestra *(Angel/EMI)*

The selection here represents a fair attempt at a history of vocal glory over the past three decades. There is, for example, the legendary Zinka Milanov in one of her best recorded performances—Leonora in *Il Trovatore*. Here she is spurred on by the equally legendary Manrico of Jussi Bjoerling. The fact that there are copious cuts observed (which are, alas, standard in most houses) and that Cellini's conducting is merely routine cannot alter the centrality of this set—nor the accomplishments of Callas and Gobbi in a spectacular *Rigoletto* nor the ravishing Victoria de los Angeles in *La Traviata* (with, however, a rather woeful supporting cast).

From more recent times there are also some noble achievements—and some failures. The *Nabucco* listed here remains the preferable version of this stirring if elemental opera. The final scene—Gobbi as Nabucco, renouncing his pagan ways and embracing the True God of Israel—is red-blooded stuff. The heroine is sung by Elena Suliotis, a Greek-born soprano on whom high hopes once rested. The reason for these hopes is audible here in the dramatic thrust of her often thrilling voice. But the Suliotis career was short-lived, and the fraying of tone that was soon to beset her is also audible in this *Nabucco* recording, made when she was still in her twenties, although it represents the best work of her tragically foreshortened career.

There is no better *Rigoletto* than the monaural Callas-Gobbi album. The Deutsche Grammophon recording listed here is the strongest of several weak contenders in stereo, and it does preserve the eloquent and powerful, if somewhat German-accented, Fischer-Dieskau performance in the title role.

Choosing the other recording of *Il Trovatore* was difficult. There is a quality in the role of Leonora that has always exactly matched the throb in Leontyne Price's voice better than any other Verdi heroine could do; yet in neither recording of the opera—this one with Mehta, or another with Herbert von Karajan conducting—has she gotten the cast she deserves.

Likewise, every ambitious diva in history, give or take a few, has sung Violetta, and most of them have recorded the role. As a solo performance, that of Victoria de los Angeles remains supreme. From later times, there is the emotion-racked Sills performance, which has the added advantage of being note-complete (as few other recordings or live performances ever are); but the Germont is weak, so that the marvelous second-act interview is undervalued. The Cotrubas-Domingo-Kleiber set is modestly successful. There is a pulling-back from the ultimate eloquence on the part of almost everyone involved, yet this is, for that very reason, a well-balanced and ultimately satisfactory performance.

Verdi: The Late Operas

Giuseppe Verdi *(1813–1901)*

Un Ballo in Maschera, *opera in three acts; text by Antonio Somma after Eugène Scribe's* Gustave III. *First performance, Rome, February 1859*

La Forza del Destino, *opera in four acts; text by Francesco Maria Piave. First performance, St. Petersburg, November 1862*

Don Carlos, *opera in five acts; text by François Joseph Méry and Camille du Locle after Schiller's play. First performance, Paris, March 1867*

Aida, *opera in four acts; text by Camille du Locle, translated into Italian by Antonio Ghislanzoni. First performance, Cairo, December 1871*

Otello, *opera in four acts; text by Arrigo Boito after Shakespeare's play* Otello. *First performance, Milan, February 1887*

Falstaff, *opera in three acts; text by Arrigo Boito after Shakespeare's* Merry Wives of Windsor. *First performance, Milan, February 1893*

During the first fourteen years of his career as a composer, Verdi created nineteen operas; during the next forty years, he composed but eight. These statistics are interesting. They do not indicate any slackening of Verdi's powers in the years after *La Traviata*—far from it. However, they do show a much greater concern with the stature of opera as an artistic entity: the remarkable thing about the eight operas of Verdi's late years is that no two of them are in any way alike. Certainly, all of them revolve in some way around the classic elements of the Italian operatic plot: some kind of love affair carried on under the burden of enormous difficulties (one of the lovers married to someone else, betrothed to someone else, or bound by loyalty to forces hostile to the other lover), which thus creates soul-shattering conflicts of patriotism, responsibility, or simply conscience. However, the contrasts in the musical materials of these operas and in the dramatic expanse they are made to fill are immense. At a time when the easy success of those nineteen earlier operas (most of them, at any rate) had already guaranteed Verdi lifelong adulation throughout the operatic world, he suddenly became obsessed with the need for moving onward. There are

Falstaff

many possible reasons, if any reason beyond mere artistic urge be needed: one, surely, is the phenomenon to the north, where the shadow of the seemingly mad innovator of opera, Richard Wagner, was like a barrier between warring musical factions. Having been told, not unkindly, that *Aida* had incorporated elements also to be found in Wagner, Verdi went into despondency and wrote no operas for six years.

No greater contrast could be imagined, for example, than that between *Un Ballo in Maschera* (The Masked Ball), written in 1859, and *La Forza del Destino* (The Power of Destiny), from three years later. The one is terse and mercurial, the most elegantly balanced of all Verdi's operas. The other is huge and sprawling: worked out like a folk epic, it tells an implausible, co-incidence-laden story of love and revenge and is

Un Ballo in Maschera

threaded through with massive choral episodes, both sacred and secular, that pull the plot (if you can call it that) in all directions at once.

Ballo is an incredible study in understated emotional torment. Verdi uses the psychologically divided stage brilliantly here. At the end of Act Two, the deceived husband Renato must learn of his wife's supposed infidelity while facing an assemblage of conspirators: his anguish in the foreground is set against the mocking laughter of the crowd as it recedes into the distance. In the next scene, in one amazing ensemble, Renato plots the murder of his rival, his errant Amelia (who loved another man but had not been unfaithful to Renato) laments her fate, and over it all is the silvery chirping of the page Oscar (sung by a coloratura soprano), who has come to invite everybody to a "splendidissimo" masked ball. The very charm and innocence of "his" singing, its spirited propulsion, makes all the more excruciating the anguish of the others.

Forza may sprawl (a complete performance can run as long as a Wagner drama), yet here, too, is music that can wrench the sensibilities. Here is Verdi reaching out for an all-embracing artwork on a single stage: the soaring passion of a wronged woman; the harsh defiance of a brother who must avenge the murder of his father; a guardian-priest who offers the solace of Heaven for what Earth can no longer abide; his comic sidekick, whose efforts to preach to a hungry crowd are mercilessly lampooned; choruses of soldiers, camp followers, monks and students. Name it, and, chances are, it's there. In its old-fashioned reliance on the power of sheer melody to tell its story, *Forza* seems to hark back somewhat to earlier

Verdi, but the melody itself is white-hot in its originality.

Don Carlos (originally in French for the Paris Opéra and later reworked into a shorter Italian version called *Don Carlo*) and *Aida* are somewhat alike in that both seem like latter-day descendants of the French grand opera of Meyerbeer—grandiose choral scenes with dance episodes, scenic display of the most lavish sort, and an intermingling of some kind of religious ceremony as a sure-fire source of mystery and exoticism. Even more important, in both works, is the effort Verdi has made to move his weighty drama constantly forward by moving ever farther away from the formalism of earlier opera (recitative leading to aria, and so on) and toward the construction of huge, musically continuous scenes.

The most stunning moment in *Don Carlos* is such a scene, a harrowing encounter between the grieving Philip II of Spain, tortured at the loss of his wife's love, and the Grand Inquisitor of Spain, whom Philip fears no less than do the lowliest of his subjects. The whole scene, set over an insistent melodic figure in the lowest instruments in the orchestra, exudes a sense of menace that can raise goosebumps. No less effective is the powerful scene late in *Aida* in which the hero Radames, an Egyptian lured into treason by his love for the enemy (Ethiopian) princess Aida, is tried and sentenced by a stern chorus, all offstage, as the frustrated Egyptian princess Amneris, who loves the hero to no avail, stands alone on the stage, shrieking helplessly into empty space.

Aida

In its affectations of exoticism (including a wonderful mumbo-jumbo consecration of sacred swords), its pageantry, and the pure hokum of its plot, *Aida* does seem like the ultimate gasp of old-fashioned grand opera. Its "Wagnerisms" consist of hardly more than an occasional use of a distinctive melodic turn-of-phrase to identify leading characters—the same device used, much more subtly and obsessively, in Richard Wagner's mature music-dramas. When Verdi determined, after *Aida,* to retire from the operatic scene, the dramatic challenge that lured him back was vastly different: the writing of William Shakespeare, fashioned into an operatic libretto by the proficient author (and composer), Arrigo Boito.

Verdi had struggled early in life with a way to express his deep reverence for Shakespeare. His *Macbeth* is more a series of illuminated episodes from the play than a reflection of the play's own line of development, but its great moments do work. Verdi also struggled, to no avail, with a setting of *King Lear.* What he lacked in earlier years, however, was a librettist to share his esteem of the Bard. Such a man he later found in Arrigo Boito, a man in whom musical and dramatic sense could combine to turn a Shakespearean drama into its own lyrical counterpart.

The result of this collaboration is a pair of operas that must for all time set a standard for the way to seek out Shakespeare's music of words and translate it into an operatic score. It takes no more than the rise of the curtain in both *Otello* and *Falstaff* to show how Boito's own theatrical sense brought out Verdi's best. For *Otello* Boito dispensed with almost all of Shakespeare's first two acts: the wooing of Othello and his Desdemona is indicated later—in flashback, so to speak—in a duet to close the first act. At the start the curtain rises on a dramatic cataclysm that tears the viewer from his seat: a gigantic storm chorus; then, immediately following, a prayer for salvation; next, without pause, the arrival of Othello at the helm of his ship and his exulting announcement of victory, followed directly by a celebration of that victory with "fires of joy" lit on the shore. *Falstaff,* too, begins in the midst of things: the fat knight is ensconced at his tavern, bullying his cohorts, preaching to them of "honor among thieves," and planning his wooing of the Merry Wives of Windsor. The first play's music uses its intense, dark power to usher in the most heartrending of romantic tragedies; that of the other is an irresistibly zestful paean to the human spirit at its most antic.

Measured against their respective plays, both operas are remarkably short. As did Mozart when teamed with da Ponte, Verdi found within himself the music to replace the words that Boito had to leave out in the transition from play to libretto. The operas are extraordinary in their range of contrast: Desdemona sings her "Ave Maria" in the final act, and as the violins mount to the top of their range to envelop the last words of the prayer, the basses sound their lowest note to usher in Otello on his dread mission; as the Queen of the Fairies invokes her troupe in the denouement of *Falstaff*—at midnight under Herne's oak tree—in stumbles the grotesque figure of the old knight himself to knock the moonbeams of the fairy chorus asunder.

Boito himself had, nearly twenty years before his collaboration with Verdi, written a decent opera in the Italian manner. This *Mefistofele,* a treatment of the Faust legend that is infinitely superior to that of Charles Gounod, holds the boards in some houses today. That work, and the uneven *La Gioconda* of Amilcare Ponchielli aside, nobody else but Giuseppe Verdi did anything to contribute toward a lasting repertory of Romantic Italian opera. When *Falstaff* was done, Verdi lived on another eight years to hear the applause of the world. Nobody, in Italy or anywhere else, ever tried to imitate his unique mastery of musical drama. When *Falstaff* was new, Giacomo Puccini was already at work. Pietro Mascagni had already enjoyed the only real operatic success of his lifetime, with his *Cavalleria Rusticana,* and Ruggiero Leoncavallo had presented *his* only opera of note, *I Pagliacci.* None of these composers owed Verdi very much of their style. Italian opera had already turned another corner.

Selected Recordings

Un Ballo in Maschera

    Maria Callas, Fedora Barbieri, Eugenia Ratti, Giuseppe di Stefano, and Tito Gobbi, with Antonio Votto and the Ensemble of La Scala *(Angel/EMI)*

    Birgit Nilsson, Giulietta Simionato, Sylvia Stahlman, Carlo Bergonzi, and Cornell MacNeil, with Sir Georg Solti and the Ensemble of Santa Cecilia, Rome *(London/Decca)*

La Forza del Destino

    Leontyne Price, Fiorenza Cossotto, Placido Domingo, Sherrill Milnes and Bonaldo Giaiotti, with James Levine and the London Symphony Orchestra *(RCA)*

    Renata Tebaldi, Giulietta Simionato, Mario del Monaco, Ettore Bastianini, and Cesare Siepi, with Francesco Molinari-Pradelli and the Ensemble of Santa Cecilia, Rome *(London/Decca)*

Don Carlo

    Montserrat Caballé, Shirley Verrett, Placido Domingo, Sherrill Milnes, and Ruggero Raimondi, with Carlo Maria Giulini and the Ensemble of the Royal Opera House, Covent Garden *(Angel/EMI)*

Aida

    Leontyne Price, Rita Gorr, Jon Vickers, and Robert

Merrill, with Sir Georg Solti and the Ensemble of the Rome Opera *(London/Decca)*

Montserrat Caballé, Fiorenza Cossotto, Placido Domingo, and Piero Cappuccilli, with Riccardo Muti and the Ensemble of the Royal Opera House, Covent Garden *(Angel/EMI)*

Otello

Mirella Freni, Jon Vickers, and Peter Glossop, with Herbert von Karajan and the Berlin Philharmonic Orchestra *(Angel/HMV)*

Herva Nelli, Ramon Vinay, and Giuseppe Valdengo, with Arturo Toscanini and the NBC Symphony Orchestra *(RCA)*

Falstaff

Ilva Ligabue, Mirella Freni, Alfredo Kraus, Geraint Evans, and Robert Merrill, with Sir Georg Solti and the Ensemble of RCA Italiana *(London/Decca)*

Ilva Ligabue, Graziella Sciutti, Juan Oncina, Dietrich Fischer-Dieskau, and Rolando Panerai, with Leonard Bernstein and the Ensemble of the Vienna State Opera *(Columbia/CBS)*

Amelia is at once the most complex and the most womanly of Verdi's heroines, and Maria Callas's realization of that places her *Ballo* recording above all competition, despite a forced tone or two in her great Act Two aria. Also in that act there is the Renato of Tito Gobbi—best of all at the moment when he becomes aware of Amelia's faithlessness—which must rank as a touchstone for the total Verdian performance. Nilsson is surprisingly feminine—or, let's at least say *womanly*—in the taut performance under Solti.

The two *Forza* performances are very nearly uncut, and that is a blessing. The ideal performance would fall somewhere between these two: it would have the throbbing richness of Leontyne Price's voice but the eloquence of Renata Tebaldi's phrasing; Mario del Monaco's ardor with Placido Domingo's freshness of tone. It basically comes down to individual preference as to which one to choose.

No recording of Verdi's original *Don Carlos* yet exists— in French, that is, and with the original first act restored complete. The marvelous, rich-textured performance under Giulini is next-best—in Italian, but with most of that first scene and with totally splendid work by the two women to make up for a certain lack of dramatic drive in the work of the three male leads.

Leontyne Price's long-time identification with Aida is more than an accident of race: she has made the part her own through the rich, plangent sense of tragedy that lies within her vocal apparatus. Vickers also has a magnificently "scenic" voice, and his work with Price, under the superlative urgency of Solti's baton, renders this performance preferable. Yet there is an ensemble quality in the newer recording under Muti that is also fine, and the Amonasro in this album is superior to the rather routine work by Robert Merrill in the Solti set.

Nobody attempts either of Verdi's two last operas without the intelligence to see into this music: these are not operas for easy success. Vickers and Karajan recreate an immense, thrusting *Otello* with which Freni and Glossop also accord well. On the other hand, since *Otello* is, after all, a conductor's score, the driving, immensely wise Toscanini performance can be endured, despite the limitations of the recording equipment of the time and the inadequacy of the cast. Both *Falstaff* recordings are brilliantly led, if a little blindingly so in Solti's case, and each has a Falstaff of consummate skill at acting through singing. In neither set is there the supreme ensemble balance that lovers of this opera dream about, but there are no performances that come any closer to perfection than these two, which are both full of sublime individual achievements by the principals.

The Waning of Romantic Opera

Georges Bizet *(1838–1875)*

Carmen, *opera in four acts; text by Henri Meilhac and Ludovic Halévy after Prosper Mérimée's novel. First performance, Paris, March 1875*

Jules Massenet *(1842–1912)*

Manon, *opera in five acts; text by Henri Meilhac and Philippe Gille based on Abbé Prévost's novel. First performance, Paris, January 1884*

Pietro Mascagni *(1863–1945)*

Cavalleria Rusticana, *opera in one act; text by Guido Menasci and Giovanni Targioni-Tozzetti after Giovanni Verga's play. First performance, Rome, May 1890*

Ruggiero Leoncavallo *(1858-1919)*

I Pagliacci, *opera in two acts; text by the composer. First performance, Milan, May 1892*

Giacomo Puccini *(1858-1924)*

La Bohème, *opera in four acts; text by Giuseppe Giacosa and Luigi Illica after Henri Murger's* Scenes of Bohemian Life. *First performance, Turin, February 1896*

Tosca, *opera in three acts; text by Giuseppe Giacosa and Luigi Illica after Victorien Sardou's play. First performance, Rome, January 1900*

Madama Butterfly, *opera in three acts; text by Giuseppe Giacosa and Luigi Illica after David Belasco's play. First performance, Milan, February 1904*

Il Trittico, *three one-act operas:* Il Tabarro, Suor Angelica *and* Gianni Schicchi; *texts by Giuseppe Adami and Giovacchino Forzano. First performance, New York, December 1918*

Turandot, *opera in three acts (completed by Franco Alfano); text by Giuseppe Adami and Renato Simoni after Carlo Gozzi's play. First performance, Milan, April 1926.*

At the very time of Giuseppe Verdi's greatest success with operatic plots of the most inflated Romantic absurdity, a major change had begun to overtake most European theater and the tastes of its audiences. The turn was to realism, the depiction of subject matter from the audience's own time and characters who were undergoing emotions similar to the audience's own—but, of course, more luridly and explicitly detailed. It was difficult for Parisian audiences, after the sensations kicked up by *Camille,* to return to the historical pageantry and chaste pastorals of an earlier time. Bad girls were decidedly in demand—best of all, if they could drag some innocent male booby down to degradation with them.

This kind of plotline did differ markedly from the taste of Verdi's audiences (for whom, after all, *La Traviata* was the one digression from type). Verdi's heroines, almost to a girl, suffered from the conflict of love and honor/duty; his plots almost always rotated around a love that crossed enemy lines, creating lyric neuroses in both hero and heroine, often to the enormous satisfaction of the "heavies" (usually the mezzo-soprano, baritone, or both).

Now we got nasty, willful girls who took their destinies

into their own hands: Carmen, willing in a moment to betray any lover for a new arrival (as she tells us in her first aria), dominating the hapless Don José as a puppeteer manipulates his dolls, almost acting out her own fate at the end as she runs onto José's outstretched knife. Thus Manon, entrapping (first innocently, later with the utmost guile) the innocent des Grieux, leaving him for the life of a prostitute, and returning only when it was too late, to die in his arms.

Georges Bizet

Jules Massenet

Thus, both Carmen and Manon came to opera as heroines from France's first literary stirrings in the direction of this new realism. Georges Bizet was already decently established as a master of a popular kind of light, somewhat sentimental operatic entertainment, of which one score, the rather pretty *Pearl Fishers,* survives. Prosper Mérimée's *Carmen* had already had a thirty-year life as a renowned literary shocker when Bizet dared to set it to music, and his setting was an important forward step in the emergence of dramatic opera—in France and in other countries as well. Bizet had never actually visited Spain, but he dug up enough of that country's national musical idiom to give his score a strong sense of locale: of the hundreds of operas by Frenchmen, Italians, Austrians, and Germans that were set in Spain, this *Carmen* of 1875 was the first to *sound* like Spain. Its exoticism, its musically brutal style (for a drama that demanded no less!) were immediately sensational, although Bizet himself died soon after his masterpiece was first unveiled to a bewildered Parisian audience.

Massenet's best works also tended to prize heavily dramatic subject matter—the havoc wrought on men's lives by the alluring Manon, the sufferings of that archetypal sad-eyed Romantic, Werther—but Massenet, for all the charm and elegance of his music, never dared as Bizet had. His best music has a faded, somewhat spineless sentimentality that only strong singers (and even stronger conductors) can overcome. Only in one opera, the *Cendrillon* (Cinderella) that is currently becoming known in opera houses after a long neglect, does the charm of Massenet assert itself relatively free from saccharine flavorings.

Pietro Mascagni

Ruggiero Leoncavallo

The passion for brutal, melodramatic plots—or, at least, a trend away from the romantic artifice that had served as operatic language for nearly a century—swept through Italy as well. Verdi's final masterpiece, *Falstaff*, was at the same time a farewell to the sublimely rational drama that Verdi had come to master. Three years before *Falstaff* a new breed of Italian opera had won its public, as exemplified by Pietro Mascagni's *Cavalleria Rusticana*, a compressed, terse drama of unmanageable brutality. Then, in 1892, Ruggiero Leoncavallo produced his masterpiece, *I Pagliacci*—again, extremely terse, compact, and beautifully constructed up to its murderous climax. Today, the two works are often paired: they add up to just about a single "normal" opera's length and give some lusty singers the chance to score in an evening, not once but twice, with extravagantly sentimental, undeniably unforgettable, big arias.

It is remarkable, in fact, that both these short operas are as heavily plotted as any full-length Romantic score—with the trappings of Romantic opera shorn away and only the central story remaining. *Cavalleria* is about the hapless Santuzza, rendered pregnant but then abandoned by the happy-go-lucky Turiddu; he then is killed in a duel occasioned by his latest philandering by, of course, the jealous husband. *Pagliacci* is an even more direct study in hot-blooded jealousy: Canio, leader of the troupe of traveling commedia dell'arte players, kills his Nedda when he discovers her infidelity—the whole action brilliantly set as a play within a play.

Giacomo Puccini

It was the near-contemporary Giacomo Puccini, however, who managed to write in this new, direct, somewhat brutal, overpoweringly sentimental style and maintain some semblance of dramatic integrity. Even so, one major advantage that rescued many moments in Puccini when pathos tended toward bathos was the composer's unfailing gift for keeping the music and the action of the plot moving along briskly. The finest of his lyric tragedies, the 1896 *La Bohème* and the 1900 *Tosca*—the one an immensely touching story of young love among the struggling artists in Paris garrets, and the other a historical play drenched in blood and the shrieks of the betrayed—are loaded with plot, yet the drama of these works is immensely enhanced by the speed of the music. The great lyric moments are brief, and the ensemble writing is tense and mercurial.

Puccini was a man of the contemporary theater: some of the most popular plays of his day were acquired for his operatic treatment almost the way Hollywood buys up prime stage properties today—and with somewhat similar results. Certainly, the lushness that Puccini brought to Sardou's *Tosca* (to fill the gap where the great French actress Sarah Bernhardt had dominated the play) and the sweetness and charming pseudo-ethnic naiveties of the operas that he based on David Belasco's plays *Madame Butterfly (Madama Butterfly)* and *The Girl of the Golden West (La Fanciulla del West)* might be taken as the precursor of the Hollywood mentality. Yet, trivial though

La Bohème

his purely musical gifts may have been, Puccini must be recognized for his stunning sense of good theater and the gesture that nails an audience to its seats. A singing actress has to be truly out of her depths if she can leave the stage at the end of *Tosca*'s second act, or fall upon her Samurai sword at the end of *Madama Butterfly,* and not leave an audience stunned beyond speech.

Late in his career Puccini created four works that must rank as the culmination of a long and active career. Three formed a "triptych" of one-act operas commissioned by the Metropolitan Opera Company and introduced in 1918: the tense, melodramatic *Il Tabarro* (The Cloak); *Suor Angelica* (Sister Angelica), with its sweet clouds of incense and its rather sentimental religious apotheosis; and *Gianni Schicchi,* a wonderful evocation of the antique farce style. The musical style of these three operas ranged farther afield than anything Puccini had tried up to then. In these works, as in *Turandot* (left unfinished at Puccini's death and completed by his disciple, Franco

Alfano), the composer becomes rather daring. It is clear, in the swirl of folklike atmosphere in *Il Tabarro* and in the mysterious, flickering choral writing in *Turandot,* that Puccini was capable of looking around at the rest of his musical world—at the music of Igor Stravinsky and Maurice Ravel, in particular—and seeing what features of that world might be adapted to his own purposes.

The tense, violent musical style that Puccini brought to high development—a style sometimes known as *verismo* (realism) because of its "trueness" to the dimensions of the story itself—was capable of infinite imitation, and Puccini left many heirs, including Mascagni, who dabbled in opera almost up to the time of his death in 1945 without ever regaining the pinnacle that *Cavalleria Rusticana* had earned him in 1890. Others among his imitators were lesser dabblers like Umberto Giordano, whose *Andrea Chénier* is still done when proper bellowers can be found for its three leading roles, and Francesco Cilea, whose *Adriana Lecouvreur* is cleverly tailored for aging sopranos looking for roles that sound harder than they are. The work of Puccini was extraordinarily popular in its time, and it remains so spellbinding today when a properly intelligent singer takes it on that it has come to represent to many audiences (and many composers) the one and only kind of art that opera should or could be. "Puccini" is still being written today; his theatrically effective style lives somewhat gracefully in such operas as Gian Carlo Menotti's *The Saint of Bleecker Street* and *Maria Golovin,* and it is still being imitated today, with somewhat less skill, by younger Americans: Carlisle Floyd (in his *Susannah* of 1956) and the even younger Thomas Pasatieri, whose fevered output grows larger by the hour.

Selected Recordings

Carmen

Teresa Berganza, Ileana Cotrubas, Placido Domingo, and Sherrill Milnes, with Claudio Abbado conducting the Ambrosian Singers and the London Symphony Orchestra *(Deutsche Grammophon)*

Victoria de los Angeles, Janine Micheau, Nicolai Gedda, and Ernest Blanc, with Sir Thomas Beecham and the French Radio Chorus and Orchestra *(Angel/EMI)*

Maria Callas, Andrea Guiot, Nicolai Gedda, and Robert Massard, with Georges Prêtre and the Paris Opera Chorus and Orchestra *(Angel/EMI)*

Manon

Victoria de los Angeles, Henri Legay, Michel Dens, and Jean Vieuille, with Pierre Monteux and the Chorus and Orchestra of the Paris Opéra-Comique *(Angel/EMI)*

Cavalleria Rusticana

Renata Scotto, Placido Domingo, and Pablo Elvira, with James Levine and the National Philharmonic Orchestra *(RCA)*

I Pagliacci

Montserrat Caballé, Placido Domingo, and Sherrill Milnes, with Nello Santi and the National Philharmonic Orchestra *(RCA)*

La Bohème

Mirella Freni, Luciano Pavarotti, Nicolai Ghiaurov, and Rolando Panerai, with Herbert von Karajan and the Berlin Philharmonic Orchestra *(London/Decca)*

Tosca

Maria Callas, Giuseppe di Stefano, and Tito Gobbi, with Victor de Sabata and the Chorus and Orchestra of La Scala *(Angel/EMI)*

Madama Butterfly

Victoria de los Angeles, Jussi Bjoerling, and Mario Sereni, with Gabriele Santini and the Rome Opera Chorus and Orchestra *(Angel/EMI)*

Il Trittico

Renata Scotto, Ileana Cotrubas, Placido Domingo, Tito Gobbi, and Ingvar Wixell, with Loren Maazel and the New Philharmonic Orchestra *(Columbia/CBS; three records available separately)*

Turandot

Birgit Nilsson, Renata Tebaldi, Jussi Bjoerling, and Giorgio Tozzi, with Erich Leinsdorf and the Rome Opera Chorus and Orchestra *(RCA/Decca)*

Not all these recordings are of the latest vintage, yet in this most performable, kindest-to-singers of all operatic repertory, there is in the above list a galaxy of stellar performances that would be worth hearing if only through a tin horn (and none of the recordings are *that* bad!). At the height of her career as an operatic singer, the great Victoria de los Angeles was the most pictorial of artists. You knew from her singing of Manon, of Carmen, and, certainly, of the wronged Madama Butterfly, exactly what the character looked like, how she felt, probably even what she was doing just before the opera began. The late

Jussi Bjoerling shared that ability: his immensely virile, brilliant, and extraordinarily ringing voice—even in the 1959 *Turandot,* which was recorded not long before his death—was a sort of celebration of the art of great singing.

The other star-among-stars in this list is, of course, Maria Callas, whose voice carried less the picture of the stage than the passion that inspired the creation of the opera itself. There are well-known moments, especially in the *Carmen* that she was probably ill-advised to try, when the luminous splendor of Callas's inner musical soul must be taken on faith, since the voice simply doesn't always do what it is supposed to do; yet to hear Callas in her first entry in *Tosca* (the earlier of the two versions she recorded) is not merely to hear a star arriving in an opera, but a dramatic moment that makes your hair stand on end.

The Abbado recording of *Carmen* has the surge of this brilliant young conductor's best work, and it is also the version closest to what Bizet himself wrote, a stark drama with the dramatic dialogue spoken rather than sung. The sung recitatives in the Callas and de los Angeles versions are not by Bizet, but by his pupil Ernest Guiraud. The two separate sets of *Cavalleria Rusticana* and *I Pagliacci* represent an extravagance. You *can* buy the two operas, in other performance versions, in one three-record set, but no "combo" has the individual qualities of Scotto's Santuzza in "Cav" or the soaring, radiant Nedda of Montserrat Caballé in the "Pag."

On the other hand, the best versions of all the separate parts of *Il Trittico (Il Tabarro, Suor Angelica,* and *Gianni Schicchi)* happen to be the three disks conducted by Loren Maazel, which have the individual advantages of Tito Gobbi's delectable Schicchi, Ileana Cotrubas to sing Lauretta's aria in that same opera, and Renata Scotto to suffer most lyrically in the two other works. Maazel, whose way with many operas seems somewhat frigid, is remarkably and atypically warm-hearted in this excellent group of separate recordings.

Supplementary Recordings

BOITO, Arrigo *(1842–1918)*
Mefistofele
Montserrat Caballé, Placido Domingo, and Norman Treigle, with Julius Rudel and the London Symphony Orchestra and Chorus *(Angel/EMI)*

PONCHIELLI, Amilcare *(1834–1886)*
　　La Gioconda
　　Renata Tebaldi, Marilyn Horne, Carlo Bergonzi, Robert Merrill, and Nicolai Ghiaurov, with Lamberto Gardelli and the Santa Cecilia Chorus and Orchestra *(London/Decca)*
CILEA, Francesco *(1866–1950)*
　　Adriana Lecouvreur
　　Renata Tebaldi, Giulietta Simionato, Mario del Monaco, and Silvio Mainico, with Franco Capuana and the Santa Cecilia Chorus and Orchestra *(London/Decca)*
MASSENET, Jules *(1842–1912)*
　　Cendrillon
　　Frederica von Stade, Ruth Welting, Jane Berbié, and Nicolai Gedda, with Julius Rudel and the Philharmonia Chorus and Orchestra *(Columbia/CBS)*

During Giuseppe Verdi's time of pre-eminence, few of his competitors attracted much attention beyond a performance or two in smaller houses. The two exceptions are listed above. Boito was a literary man of high skill, who collaborated with Verdi as librettist on his two Shakespearean masterpieces (and on the revision of several earlier librettos as well). On his own, Boito was a prolific composer, working in a broad, grandiose manner that occasionally stretched toward new musical horizons. His masterpiece, beyond question, is the *Mefistofele* of 1868—nine years after the *Faust* of Gounod and immensely more Faustian in its treatment of both the romance and the mystery in the score. The late Norman Treigle enjoyed his greatest triumph in the diabolical title role of the opera, and the excellent Angel performance preserves the panache that he brought to the score.

Ponchielli's foolish, convoluted melodrama (whose libretto was written by Boito under a pseudonym) is best known for its "Dance of the Hours" ballet; but it makes up for musical thinness by being exceptionally well-written for show-off singers, and the Tebaldi-Horne-Bergonzi recording is filled with daredevil vocalizing of little subtlety but enormous flamboyance. There is no other reason for reviving *La Gioconda* than for performing it in this way.

A far inferior work, Cilea's *Adriana Lecouvreur,* also descends from *La Gioconda.* It works up a kind of specious surface drama—involving a famous historic character, the French actress of the same name, and a fictitious rivalry that results in her death. It is also easier to sing than it sounds, and so its pallid, derivative score is much beloved by singers somewhat over the hill. Even at its advanced age, it is very much like a lot of bad Puccini rewrites that pass for new opera today (by the likes of Menotti, Pasatieri, the late Vittorio Giannini, and others).

More rewarding than any of these is the Cinderella opera of Massenet, written with a charm and an elegance so different from the saccharine of *Manon* and *Werther* that it shouldn't even be listed in their company. The opera has recently been revived extensively, thanks largely to the lovely talents of the young American mezzo-soprano Frederica von Stade. This recording preserves the extraordinary charm of her musical personality: the score has been somewhat altered to give the prince's role to a tenor (instead of a female voice, as written), but there is enough stylishness in the performance overall to atone for this minor mischief.

4.
Wagner and the Language of Symbolism

The notion of combining music and drama into a single artistic expression goes back, as we've already seen, to just around the start of the seventeenth century. From that time forward for a good 250 years, the great composers of musical drama worked with full awareness of the tastes of their audiences. Whatever mystique we may wrap around the institution of opera today, the works of the great Italian and French masters, from Monteverdi to Verdi, Rameau to Massenet, were conceived as the most dazzling popular theatrical entertainment of their day. The latest operatic tunes of Mozart, like those of Bizet and Puccini, were sung in cafés and whistled on the streets; the great singers of the time were lionized the way movie stars are today.

Richard Wagner

Only one major figure in the history of music drama dared to challenge the notion of that art as popular entertainment, and that figure happened to be a genius of astounding attainment: Richard Wagner. Born in a Germany torn by political unrest, province against province, ideology against despotic fiat, Wagner found his own sense of nationality in the growing artistic language of his country: the folk-operas of Weber and his followers and, above all, the purely Germanic heroism that Beethoven translated into music—not only in his opera *Fidelio* but also into the Ninth Symphony, which reaches a point where mere orchestral expression can go no farther and resolves that dilemma by bursting into song, German song, the "Ode to Joy" of Friedrich Schiller. The revolutionary spirit in Wagner's own conscience took from Beethoven's own fearlessness a license to do what one wanted to do, regardless of the consequences. The egomaniac in Wagner's psyche fanned the flame. Wagner was the first to proclaim himself a genius, and to stipulate what the world therefore owed him.

But for one thing, Wagner would have gone down in history as merely the greatest con artist of all time. He conned friend and foe, monarch and manservant, into providing him with his every need: an opera house (nay, shrine) in which to parade his genius; a press to circulate his manic, self-serving manifestoes; any woman who took his fancy to warm his bed, married or not. That one thing, that quality that made the price Wagner exacted not one cent too high, is the quality of the artwork he produced. Wagner's pronouncements surrounding his mature creations may have resounded in accents of madness, but as a composer, Richard Wagner was every bit as good as he thought he was. He was driven by a vision of a level of art that had never existed before, and he came close enough to attaining that level so that his creative energy wrought profound changes in the art of his time. He was, in other words, an innovator with a most profound impact.

Beyond the stature of the works themselves, Wagner's innovations forced upon the world a rethinking of the relationship between the work of art and the consumer. His abilities as a master showman cannot be questioned, yet he shrank with loathing from the notion that the Muse he served was merely the progenitor of pleasant listening. He demanded from his audiences participation in the realization of what he put on his stage: they had to listen, feel, and think. His plots were interlaced with musical and dramatic symbols, and the audience was expected to pay strict attention to the way these symbols guided the course of the drama. It wasn't merely that he devised a system of "leitmotives," musical calling-cards to identify the characters in his dramas and their props and gadgetry—a motive for Siegfried, for example, and another for his sword: these motives underwent musical changes from one context to another, and the audience was expected to grasp these subtleties and use them as a guide through the immense tangle of words and music that constitutes a Wagnerian texture.

Thus, Wagner's Bayreuth, the musical theater built to his specifications by his royal patron Ludwig II of Bavaria, was not merely a place of diversion, as were the great opera houses of France, Italy, England, and America: it was a pilgrim's goal. His music became, in his lifetime and in the years that followed, the center of a cult. The music was hated as widely as it was loved; it stirred every known emotion except apathy.

In this very fact, Wagner's musical contributions changed the world—at least the operatic world. When he died in 1883, shortly after the completion of the most mystical, and therefore most mysterious, of all his dramas, the "consecrational stage-ritual" *Parsifal,* the world was swept by a concern as to who would succeed him. Nobody ever did, but many tried. The young Richard Strauss, whose father had played under Wagner at Munich and Bayreuth, attempted to emulate a Wagnerian kind of symbolism, a meaning beneath meaning, an appeal to an audience's appetite for serious artistic mental exercises; yet Strauss's most successful opera was *Der Rosenkavalier,* the one in which his campaign to assume Wagner's mantle was momentarily replaced by a skillful stab at quasi-Mozartian comedy. The Frenchman Claude Debussy was one contemporary composer whose writings struck out bitterly at the Wagnerian shadow that had fallen across so much music; his immensely quiet, mysterious master-piece *Pelléas et Mélisande* was one of the few works that attained Wagner's fusion of music, theater, and under-stated subtleties.

Of those who willingly accepted Wagner as musical progenitor, few were involved with opera. The nine symphonies of Anton Bruckner are seldom more than wide-eyed, naive love-letters to the titan of Bayreuth. Gustav Mahler's gigantic orchestral output also reflects, in somewhat more imaginative ways, the implications of Wagner's harmony, and so, of course, do the works of the Viennese atonalists—Arnold Schoenberg, Anton Webern, and Alban Berg—who attempted their own musical reso-lution in the early decades of the twentieth century, while drawing much succor from the musical language of *Tristan und Isolde.* It would perhaps be stretching a point to impute a direct line to Wagnerian music drama in the two masterful operas of Alban Berg, *Wozzeck* and the unfinished *Lulu;* yet the Wagnerian shadow falls upon these works, even at some distance, and it is one of those amusing if useless parlor games to try to decide where the musical world would be today if Richard Wagner hadn't passed through it at one time.

Wagner: The Early Operas

Richard Wagner *(1813–1883)*

The Flying Dutchman, *opera in three acts; text after Heinrich Heine's* Memoirs of Von Schnabelewopski. *First performance, Dresden, January 1843*
Tannhäuser, *opera in three acts. First performance, Dres-den, October 1845*

Lohengrin, *opera in three acts. First performance, Weimar, August 1850*

The young revolutionary Wagner traveled widely and desperately, hounded by enemies both political and musical, both real and imagined. He supported himself where he could, conducting in the pits of provincial opera houses, scribbling music for publishers for little more than subsistence pay. However, his work as a conductor did him much good: he built a musical philosophy out of an assimilation of the best and a denial of the worst in his forebears. Wagner's earliest operas would not be known at all today, except for their stature as the apprentice work of a future genius: *The Fairies,* a comedy with supernatural overtones that was clearly beholden to Weber and Marschner; *Forbidden Love,* a Mendelssohnian paraphrase of Shakespeare's *Measure for Measure; Rienzi,* an attempt to imitate the grand, if grandiose, manner of Meyerbeer.

Then came *The Flying Dutchman,* the first opera we can hear for the surge of its music and for the promise of the Wagner to come. Again the inspiration is Weber—the surging sea-music, the almost blinding gleam of the music for the purer-than-pure heroine, the ghostly choruses of the Dutchman's crew of dead men. By the standards of the later Wagner, this is old-fashioned stuff, full of songs and episodes; but the composer of this tingling, vivid music needs no apology.

The *Dutchman* was the last of Wagner's works to be inspired by a specific outside literary source, in this case a poetic journal of Heinrich Heine. Yet, as Wagner himself reworked Heine's text, elements that would figure as Wagnerian concerns were brought to the fore, most of all the theme of redemption. The Dutchman is redeemed from his ordained exile by the pure love of Senta. Then, when Senta seems (at least to the Dutchman) to waver in her purity, he must resume his exile. But Senta has remained pure, and she jumps to her death to prove it, whereupon both she and the Dutchman are redeemed, transfigured Heavenward, their earthly journey finally ended.

The theme of redemption remained uppermost in every ensuing work. Elsa, beloved of Lohengrin, wavers in her faith but finds redemption in Lohengrin's own sacrifice. Tannhäuser, stained morally by his dalliance in the halls of Venus, is redeemed by his pure love of

Elisabeth—its purity again underlined by her death. Later on, the final notes of the titanic *Ring* cycle, after its allegory of the rise and fall of Mankind has been acted out and the world purified by the flames that engulf the mountain of the gods—those final notes sound the theme of promise, the leitmotive of Redemption Through Love. The love of Tristan and Isolde, denied earthly existence due to prior commitments, is preserved for another existence on a higher plane as the lovers' death redeems them both. And in *Parsifal*, the last music Wagner was to write, the cleansing power of faith, the purity of the "guileless fool" who brings back to earth the tools of its salvation, is the redemption of us all—and, most likely, of the tarnished soul of Wagner himself.

From *The Flying Dutchman* on, each new work was for Wagner a mighty step forward in the formation of a set of precepts that he never foreswore. In both *Tannhäuser* and *Lohengrin* the very settings represent one major Wagnerian concern: Germany, or Germanic land, and its fund of ancient legend out of which a new art could be born. *Tannhäuser* is well stocked with authentic German personages—the great singer-poets who gave Germany its heritage of song. It is in a song contest that his hero is betrayed: in a sense the battle over Tannhäuser's soul is the struggle between sacred and profane music that Wagner was to re-express in jollier tones in *Die Meistersinger*.

Lohengrin

Yet, Tannhäuser, too, is old-fashioned in one sense. It is made up of short, finite scenes, songs with beginnings and ends, the paraphernalia of traditional opera. Something else, however, was taking shape in Wagner's own imagination: a new kind of flowing artistic language, words welded inseparably to music, reaching no full cadences merely for the purpose of letting the audience applaud but flowing inexorably forward with the drama. In *Lohengrin* this began to happen. What also happens is that much of the music becomes a handmaiden of drama in the form of the leitmotive, the recurring musical theme that identifies a character or his/her paraphernalia in Wagnerian opera.

Lohengrin appears as the savior of the innocent Elsa. She must never ask him his name or whence he comes, he tells her, and this orchestral phrase, stentorian and terse, echoes through later scenes as Elsa becomes prey to her curiosity. The rich, robust orchestration and the massive expanse of the dramatic rhetoric fashion from *Lohengrin* something close to a masterpiece. Only the greatest musicians, of course, can fill it with the life-force that can keep it from seeming rather slow, at least on the surface.

Selected Recordings

The Flying Dutchman
> Janis Martin, René Kollo, Norman Bailey, and Martti Talvela, with Sir Georg Solti and the Chicago Symphony Orchestra and Chorus *(London/Decca)*

Tannhäuser
> Helga Dernesch, Christa Ludwig, René Kollo, Hans Sotin, and Victor Braun, with Sir Georg Solti and the Vienna Philharmonic Chorus and Orchestra *(London/Decca)*

> Elisabeth Grümmer, Marianne Schech, Hans Hopf, Gottlob Frick, and Dietrich Fischer-Dieskau, with Franz Konwitschny and the German State Opera *(Angel/EMI)*

Lohengrin
> Elisabeth Grümmer, Christa Ludwig, Jess Thomas, and Dietrich Fischer-Dieskau, with Rudolf Kempe and the Vienna Philharmonic Orchestra and Chorus *(Angel/EMI)*

The preferred *Dutchman* takes precedence not only because of the magnificent surge of Solti's leadership and the exceptionally powerful work of the British baritone Norman Bailey in the title role, but also because it is performed as originally written by Wagner—as one continuous act in three scenes. Surely as short a work as this must benefit by this mode of treatment. Most impresarios, when asked why they give the *Dutchman* in three acts, will mumble something about the bar in the opera house needing the intermission business.

The two *Tannhäuser* recordings use, respectively, the Paris revision and the original Dresden version. The Paris revision, which includes the full Venusberg Bacchanale, also benefits from the hand of a surer Wagner, sixteen years later, recognizing many dull or unworkable passages and making drastic changes. There are, of course, the potent arguments of Grümmer's radiant Elisabeth and Fischer-Dieskau as the Wolfram of our dreams in the

Dresden recording, although this argument is somewhat offset by Kollo's Tannhäuser under Solti, a marvelously vivid portrayal of a role so easily made boring by others (Hans Hopf among them).

The single *Lohengrin* listed is not bad, except for some woolly moments from Thomas in the title role. There really isn't any competition at this writing, however: there is a 1962 performance from Bayreuth, another from 1953, and one from Tanglewood—each with at least one major role sung unspeakably badly. The version listed, at least, has the splendor of Grümmer, once again, as the heroine.

Wagner: The Ring of the Nibelungen

Das Rheingold, *prologue in one act. First performance, Munich, September 1869*
Die Walküre, *music drama in three acts. First performance, Munich, June 1870*
Siegfried, *music drama in three acts. First performance, August 1876*
Götterdämmerung, *music drama in a prologue and three acts. First performance, August 1876*

Drawing upon a thicket of ancient Germanic and Nordic legend, Wagner fashioned a drama about nothing less than the rise and fall of humankind. The impulse did not arrive overnight; as early as 1848 he struggled with a text that dealt only with the death of the world-hero Siegfried. As that took shape, however, Wagner increasingly saw the need to go farther back, and then farther still, in telling the story of the gold treacherously wrested from the Rhine maidens and forged into a ring whose owner would rule the world; of the mating of the twins Siegmund and Sieglinde, children of Wotan, to produce the hero Siegfried; of the mating of Siegfried with Brünnhilde (his aunt, it so happens); of Brünnhilde's betrayal of Siegfried; and of Siegfried's death as the gods' Valhalla perishes in flames.

The impact and implications of this most titanic of all musical creations has been extensively written about by essayists like George Bernard Shaw *(The Perfect Wagnerite)* and by responsible biographers like Ernest Newman and Robert Gutman. There remains the music. Not until the mid-1960s was there a complete recorded traversal of this music: now we are engulfed in a confusion of choice. Hearing the music away from a stage production, allowing the mind to be flooded by the intense pictorialism of the music, is probably superior to enduring the run-of-the-mill stagings current in opera houses around the world, whether in the literal picture-postcard style of most new American stagings or the chic, super-symbolic renderings that have now taken over at Bayreuth. Beyond question, Wagner would have availed himself of the latest media gadgetry had he been writing this music in more recent times.

Hearing the music, one can easily forget to breathe. Much of this is Wagner's doing, his realization of what he called "endless melody"—a way of writing in which the music seems never to come to a point of harmonic rest. In later works—*Tristan und Isolde* most of all—this onrushing harmonic instability tends to destroy all sense of being in any given key. That doesn't happen in *The Ring*, however. What does happen is an interaction between listener and music that is somewhat similar to floating, free of gravity, free of the framework of time as we usually know it. It might be possible to experience Wagner's *Ring* as background while doing something else. It would be a feat of enormous difficulty, and one would be foolish to attempt it.

Selected Recordings

Complete Cycles

Birgit Nilsson, Wolfgang Windgassen, Kirsten Flagstad, Christa Ludwig, James King, and Gustav Neidlinger, with Sir Georg Solti and the Vienna State Opera Chorus and Orchestra *(London/Decca)*

Régine Crespin, Helga Dernesch, Helge Brilioth, Josephine Veasey, Dietrich Fischer-Dieskau, and Thomas Stewart, with Herbert von Karajan and the Berlin State Opera Chorus and Berlin Philharmonic Orchestra *(Deutsche Grammophon)*

Martha Mödl, Ludwig Suthaus, Ferdinand Frantz, Georgine von Milinkovic, Ira Malaniuk, and Julius Patzak, with Wilhelm Furtwängler and the RAI Chorus and Rome Symphony Orchestra *(Seraphim)*

Rita Hunter, Alberto Remedios, Norman Bailey, Derek Hammond-Stroud, Katherine Pring, and Gregory Dempsey, with Reginald Goodall and the English National Opera *(Angel/EMI)*

When it was completed in 1965, the Solti traversal of the *Ring* was hailed as the most distinguished achievement by the record industry to date, and the distinction may still apply, even with the wealth of alternatives now available. Solti's grasp of the score was (and remains) tremendously spirited and colorful: the sweep of his work, abetted by the magnificence of the Viennese performers and the splendor of the recorded sound, is as close to irresistible as the devout Wagnerian might wish. The Karajan performance, however, has its fervent admirers also. Their argument rests primarily on the impact of Karajan's own original, creative spirit on the music and his obvious attempt to "translate" the massive proportions of the music down to living-room size. The Furtwängler recording dates from 1953 and was captured from radio tapes made in Rome. The sound, although monaural, is clear enough for the listener to recognize that conductor as one of the great creative spirits of our century. The Goodall performance uses the extremely attractive new English translation by Andrew Porter, and Goodall himself is the vital force in a vivid performance that certainly stands on its own merits.

Among the singers' performances, there are sublime moments: Jon Vickers, the Siegmund in the Karajan set, will send chills up anyone's spine with his appeal to his father, Wälse, in Act One of *Die Walküre*, and so will Birgit Nilsson's final scene in the Solti *Götterdämmerung*. There are shaky moments here and there in all the sets, as the mere law of averages would suggest in a survey across seventy-six long-playing discs! The hooty Brünnhilde of Martha Mödl in the Furtwängler set takes some getting used to, as does the Siegfried of Albert Remedios in the English-language version. Nevertheless, as these words are written to suggest, a recording of the *Ring* cycle is an indispensable item for any serious collection, and nobody undertakes to perform this music without something in mind. It is thus impossible to go drastically wrong with any of these titanic recordings.

Wagner: The Late Works

Tristan und Isolde, *music drama in three acts. First performance, Munich, June 1865*
Die Meistersinger von Nürnberg, *music drama in three acts. First performance, Munich, June 1868*

Parsifal, *consecrational music drama in three acts. First performance, Bayreuth, July 1882*

agner did not attempt to hide the source of his inspiration for *Tristan und Isolde.* He conceived this drama about frustrated love, based on Celtic legend, while he was a guest at the home of his friend Otto Wesendonck and was simultaneously carrying on a clandestine affair with Wesendonck's wife Mathilde.

No opera in existence so completely joins music and dramatic theme. The broad expansion of the harmonic language, which Wagner had already begun to suggest in *Lohengrin* and in the *Ring,* becomes in *Tristan* a challenge to one of music's basic tenets—that music must be framed within a distinct tonality. In *Tristan,* unresolved harmonic implications become a symbol of unrequited love, and the analogy works uncommonly well. The scheme of the leitmotive, so pictorially used in the *Ring,* here becomes a set of psychological transformations.

As *Tristan* works on this level of frustration and thwarted hopes, it takes on the form of a vast symphony in the most classic sense. The music that expresses the culmination of the lovers' passion in Act Two, interrupted as they are discovered by the duped husband, is sung again later by the dying Isolde, and this time it is sung to its conclusion. What was thwarted in life, musically and dramatically, therefore becomes realized in death. From such suggestions is this most personal of musical dramas suspended.

Was *Die Meistersinger,* which followed *Tristan,* some sort of purge, self-administered? The thought probably didn't occur to Wagner, nor should it detain us here. The fact remains, though, that the supremely rational comedy of *Die Meistersinger* marked a return by Wagner to human drama while his musical style turned once again to a celebration of basic harmonic values. Surely this most marvelous of comedies is not in any sense a regression on Wagner's part. What is more likely is that the story Wagner wanted to tell is his own: a young poet-singer has his artistic wings momentarily clipped by pedants who would suppress innovation, but his quest is furthered by a wise older poet. Wagner probably wished the allegory to be made as clear as possible. In doing so, however, he wrote a most un-pedantic tract in which the beauty of the characters themselves becomes the source for the radiant beauty of the music.

In this one work the entire populace consists of humans—no saints, demons or Nordic gods, no motivation of plot through potions or manifestations. Hans Sachs, the poet-cobbler, actually existed in medieval Germany, and in his championing the "new art" of the ardent young hero Walter von Stolzing, Wagner turns Sachs into an eloquent apologist for himself. Just as apparent, the villain Beckmesser, the pedant who claims that all art must adhere to ancient and outmoded rules, is the personification of the critic Eduard Hanslick, who himself fought all forms of Wagnerism.

Less clear by far are the motivations for the final drama, a celebration of the legend of the Holy Grail set to music by a composer among whose many flaws atheism was one of the least flagrant. To reckon the work an act of expiation would be unrealistic. It is far more likely that Wagner had come to find in himself a vast treasury of solemn, fragile, immensely slow-moving devotional music. Like the earlier *Tannhäuser,* the crux of *Parsifal* is the

Parsifal

battle between sacred and profane love; yet in this last work, the hero—and thus the world—is triumphant.

Parsifal is a forbidding work for reasons other than its solemnity. It is Wagner's own journey to the brink of musical chaos. Here again, as in *Tristan,* ties once considered basic to a musical rationale are readily dissolved. It is impossible to hear such a passage as the Prelude to Act Three of *Parsifal* as a work in the mainstream of harmonic practice. The music has been set free to seek out a new language. Perhaps it is that new freedom that *Parsifal* actually seeks to consecrate. A generation of composers who followed in Wagner's shadow seem to have thought so.

Selected Recordings

Tristan und Isolde

Kirsten Flagstad, Ludwig Suthaus, and Dietrich Fischer-Dieskau, with Wilhelm Furtwängler and the Philharmonia Orchestra *(Angel/EMI)*

Helga Dernesch, Jon Vickers, and Walter Berry, with Herbert von Karajan and the Berlin Philharmonic Orchestra *(Deutsche Grammophon)*

Die Meistersinger

Caterina Ligendza, Placido Domingo, Dietrich Fischer-Dieskau, and Roland Hermann, with Eugen Jochum and the German Opera Chorus and Orchestra *(Deutsche Grammophon)*

Helen Donath, René Kollo, Theo Adam, and Sir Geraint Evans, with Herbert von Karajan and the Dresden State Opera *(Angel/EMI)*

Parsifal

Gwyneth Jones, James King, Franz Crass, and Thomas Stewart, with Pierre Boulez and the 1970 Bayreuth Festival *(Deutsche Grammophon)*

Christa Ludwig, René Kollo, Gottlob Frick, and Dietrich Fischer-Dieskau, with Sir Georg Solti and the Vienna Philharmonic Chorus and Orchestra *(London/ Decca)*

Those who remember Kirsten Flagstad as the greatest of Isoldes will take comfort from the burning spirit that infuses this complete recorded collaboration with Wilhelm Furtwängler, the moderately good Ludwig Suthaus, and the very young (but eloquent) Dietrich Fischer-Dieskau. The recording is old, and in mono, but there is something so vivid about the performance that the album must rank among the great recorded achievements of any era. This said, the elegance and intensity of the newer Karajan album should disappoint few, and the Tristan of Jon Vickers is another incandescent creation that demands careful hearing.

The two competing *Meistersinger* performances are

admirable, with the great strength of Jochum's conducting and the marvelous Sachs of Fischer-Dieskau combining to give that recording a slight edge. Yet Solti's performance has its points, especially the liveliness and wit of the conception and the hilarious yet totally human Beckmesser of Evans.

The Ring of the Niebelungen

Ardent Wagnerites may be startled by the clarity of the Boulez performance of *Parsifal* from Bayreuth, but it is a fascinating performance that etches in stunning relief the elements in this score that point the way clearly ahead (to the modern age in which Boulez himself figures so strongly). Solti's performance moves along traditional lines, but at least it moves, and the singing—by the splendidly fresh-voiced Kollo, most of all—is first-rate. That, alas, cannot be said for the cast under Boulez, fascinating though his overall conception might be.

After Wagner

Richard Strauss *(1864–1949)*

Salomé, *opera in one act; text by Hedwig Lachmann after Oscar Wilde's play. First performance, Dresden, December 1905*

Der Rosenkavalier, *opera in three acts; text by Hugo von Hofmannsthal. First performance, Dresden, January 1911*

Claude Debussy *(1862-1918)*

Pelléas et Mélisande. *opera in five acts, text by Maurice Maeterlinck from his play. First performance, Paris, April 1902*

Alban Berg *(1885-1935)*

Wozzeck, *opera in three acts, fifteen scenes; text by Berg after the play by Georg Büchner. First performance, Berlin, December 1925*
Lulu, *opera in three acts; text by Berg after two plays by Frank Wedekind. Left unfinished at the composer's death. First performance in the unfinished, two-act form, Zurich, June 1937. First performance of the opera as completed from Berg's sketches by Friedrich Cerha, Paris, March 1979*

One of the lesser legacies of Richard Wagner was the imposition onto music of an air of mystery and the suspicion that this most arcane of all arts must follow a path predetermined by some higher power. Before Wagner, composers for the most part busied themselves by merely writing music, and audiences busied themselves enjoying that music or rebelling against it. Now, from the shrine at Bayreuth came the seeming dictum that all music must be approached as a holiness. That is one reason that some members of today's audiences tend to feel some secret guilt at the possibility that they are actually having a good time in the presence of the Great Masters. That, of course, is sheer nonsense, but Wagner apparently had a strong taste for absorbing nonsense and proclaiming it with all the sacrosanctity of a latter-day Sermon on the Mount.

Thus, it happened that upon Wagner's passing a great cry went up about who would succeed to the throne that the composer himself and others had bestowed upon Wagner. In Germany, at first, and even beyond its borders into France and elsewhere, it wouldn't do for a composer, around 1900, to be measured for the quality of his art: he must stand measurement as to his fitness to become the "next Wagner."

Richard Strauss grew up in the Wagnerian shadow: his father even played French horn under Wagner's direction. Strauss's earliest successes were a series of garish orchestral tone-poems in which a Wagnerian mystique and the Wagnerian leitmotive technique were stretched and shortened to fit the Procrustean bed of orchestral language. These works (*Also sprach Zarathustra*, and *Ein Heldenleben*, to name a couple) still hold their place when a properly flamboyant interpretation can produce a brave noise. However, by the turn of the century, Strauss had made his commitment to opera, and this was the field he was to toil in for most of his long life.

Salomé

Strauss's operatic skills were indeed vast and fascinating in their command of sheer theatrical insight: in this his music resembles that of the less flamboyant Giacomo Puccini. As a successor to Wagner, however, his failings were inevitably apparent. Yes, he, too, wrote brilliant music for a large orchestra, on which the vocal line floated for some time, became submerged for some time, and occasionally formed an approximate union; but Strauss had little interest in either Wagner's ardent drive to move artistic frontiers forward or his need to invest his music with more than its overtly musical values. Strauss was therefore a composer in the operatic mainstream, concerned most of all with entertaining and reasonably shrewd in employing toward that end the most fashionable artistic devices of his time.

His first great success was the tense, brilliantly colored setting of the *Salomé* of Oscar Wilde. It is a terse, devastatingly brutal work in a single act lasting about one hundred minutes, and Strauss never wrote anything more innovative than this work of his relative youth. Musically, *Salomé* is far more conservative than late Wagner. Its harmony harks back to composers like Schumann and Mendelssohn, although Strauss very cleverly works in a thin frosting of dissonance to hide the conservatism of his style. What makes *Salomé* work so well is its amazing range of color, the virtuosity of its orchestral effects (for example, the eerie harmonic on a solo string bass as John the Baptist is decapitated—offstage, you'll be happy to learn—or the fetid growl from flutes at the low end of their range as Salomé lies in her final ecstasy, making love to that severed head). For the most part, there is no vocal line to remember, but merely an extremely clever use of the voice in jagged, strained writing to illustrate the extreme emotion of the plot.

At the other end of the Straussian gamut is his most popular opera, *Der Rosenkavalier,* a most elegant comedy of manners that is set in the Vienna of Mozart and fondly imagines itself to be an evocation of that earlier master's spirit. It is no such thing, of course. Even granting the 125 years that separate the two men's works, you need only contrast the parodied love-making in the final scene of *Figaro* with the burlesque scene in which the loutish Baron Ochs woos the supposed chambermaid in Strauss's opera to sense the difference in expressive levels.

This would not matter in our approach to *Der Rosenkavalier* if Strauss himself did not rub our noses in it. In his letters, and in certain external aspects of his writing, he subpoenas the ghost of Mozart to his side and thereby shames himself. *Der Rosenkavalier* is a work of exceptional prettiness. Stringing a suite of pseudo-Viennese waltzes through the score may be anachronistic in a work set around 1760, but these dances are so brilliantly conceived that they serve as an added, valuable level of humor. The sheer virtuosity of the final scene, a trio for women's voices wreathed in the most fragrant writing for high strings, bespeaks a composer whom we cannot neglect; and the trailing-off of that trio into the last music, the sweetest of folk songs, to cap this four-hour parade of sentiment, tragedy, elegance, and burlesque, is another master stroke. Yet nowhere in the work, despite the composer's fond imaginings, does Mozart appear.

Strauss spent most of his later career reworking the

charms of *Der Rosenkavalier* into other contexts *(Arabella, Capriccio,* and others). The brutality of *Salomé* also motivated *Elektra* and the excruciatingly protracted *Die Frau ohne Schatten,* a symbolistic tangle that no rational plot analysis can untangle. It is clear that, like many another tragic figure who long outlived his greatest success (Mascagni's name comes first to mind), Strauss would be far more honored today if he had only known when to stop.

Yet Strauss was the last of Germany's composers to enjoy popular acceptance in his time. Even as he struggled to keep alive the lessons of his nation's musical tradition, there were others nearby who, in the eyes of the crowd at least, sought to destroy it. Reacting with far greater insight to the implications of Wagner's *Tristan* and *Parsifal,* the Viennese Arnold Schoenberg and his disciples turned out both music and broadsides that asked basic and frightening questions: Why must music hew to a central tonality? Why define *tune* in Mozartian terms? Why stand still?

Wagner had, in *Tristan* most of all, demonstrated how a deliberate obscuring of harmonic direction, an evasion of expected cadences, became a part of the drama of frustration that his music was to serve. In 1925 a disciple of Schoenberg, Alban Berg, produced his *Wozzeck,* an opera in which the questions asked by his teacher were answered in a brilliant and harrowing form.

Alban Berg

The play had been written nearly a century before, by the tortured boy-genius Georg Büchner (1813–37), an amazing story for its time about the destruction of the common man by a world of mechanized near-maniacs. Berg seized upon the play and set it to music of remarkable power and variety. The common soldier Wozzeck and his mistress Marie are musically defined in a style clearly derived from Wagner, via Gustav Mahler; the nameless personages of the uncomprehending world around them become grotesques in music cut loose from tonality, itself manic and amorphous. To contain the richness of this variety, Berg hit upon the scheme of imposing upon the opera an overall symphonic plan: each scene is in a form derived from instrumental music, and the whole is bound by a tense, classical logic. Even here, Berg's device is directly descended from Wagner's *Tristan*, where, too, the apotheosis is like a symphonic exegesis of the thwarted love music earlier on.

Berg died with his final opera incomplete, but this *Lulu* has now been completed from the composer's voluminous sketches. Lulu, a creation of the Expressionist playwright Frank Wedekind, is perhaps the ultimate human symbol, the personification of lust and greed—yet also of joy and transfiguration—in a woman who lives beyond morality. With the completed *Lulu* at hand, it is obvious that here, too, Berg used as his framework a formal, perhaps symphonic form. The opera is in two halves that work as mirror-images: up to a point Lulu destroys through love, and beyond that lies her own destruction.

That is not, of course, the way we listen to the work. As a drama purposely fashioned to work outside human reactions, *Lulu* was used by Berg to express completely the strength of music beyond the harmonic strictures of the previous four or more centuries. So brilliant is the joining of music and drama that it is possible to hear *Lulu* and come away convinced of the logic—even the strange, if fetid, beauty—of this abstruse musical language.

Claude Debussy

However, three decades before, Claude Debussy had accomplished something not entirely dissimilar in his one opera, which may well have been his greatest work. Maurice Maeterlinck's play, *Pelléas et Mélisande*, is, once again, a drama of half-lights and incompleted, superficially irrational actions. The child-like Mélisande comes from nowhere. Like Lulu, she is a creature beyond morality—but this time out of innocence, not guilt. Her dalliance with Pelléas, her husband's half-brother, is seen by her as perfectly natural; a nameless Fate moves all characters in the drama together or apart.

For this Debussy's music is, in its own way, as purposefully inconclusive as that of Berg. Outwardly, Debussy resisted the implications of Wagnerism, but *Pelléas et Mélisande* is a quiet, half-lit kin to *Tristan,* not only in its plot, but also in the way a shroud of elusive, haunting, sometimes almost unbearably rapturous music seems to envelop the unstated, poignant drama. Also, as in *Tristan,* the voices in *Pelléas* seem to float on a fully realized orchestral texture, intoning a drama, not as vocal virtuosity, but as a series of secret messages to the audience.

Selected Recordings

Salomé

 Birgit Nilsson, Gerhard Stolze, and Eberhard Waechter, with Sir Georg Solti and the Vienna Philharmonic Orchestra *(London)*

 Hildegard Behrens, Karl-Walter Böhm, and José van Dam, with Herbert von Karajan and the Vienna Philharmonic Orchestra *(Angel/EMI)*

Der Rosenkavalier

 Elisabeth Schwarzkopf, Christa Ludwig, and Otto Edelmann, with Herbert von Karajan and the Philharmonic Orchestra *(Angel/EMI)*

Wozzeck

 Walter Berry, Fritz Uhl, and Isabel Strauss, with Pierre Boulez and the Paris Opera Orchestra *(Columbia/CBS)*

Lulu

 Teresa Stratas, Yvonne Minton, Robert Tear, and Kenneth Riegel, with Pierre Boulez and the Paris Opera Orchestra *(Deutsche Grammophon)*

Pelléas et Mélisande

 Erna Spoorenberg, Camille Mauranne, and George London, with Ernest Ansermet and the Suisse Romande Orchestra *(London/Decca)*

The razor edge of Nilsson's Salomé, a thrill not to be forgotten by those who experienced it in an opera house, forces even Solti into the shadows in the phenomenal London recording, although the sound is no longer new. The excellent Karajan performance has a less sensational —but, just possibly, more responsibly musical—Salomé in Hildegard Behrens, and the set as a whole is a more balanced performance. It is a matter of personal opinion as to whether that is an ideal for a performance of Salomé : the opera seems to work best when still rather raw.

There are newer recordings than the Schwarzkopf-Karajan *Rosenkavalier,* but none with a heroine who draws the tears as Schwarzkopf does at every moment when she holds the stage. Edelmann's Ochs is rather bullish, against the librettist's wishes; there is more music in the Walter Berry performance on Columbia, in spite of Leonard Bernstein's wretched mangling of the score. Nevertheless, the set of choice here, with certain flaws acknowledged, is one of those glowing achievements that makes collecting records a privilege.

No contemporary conductor unravels the intricacy of Berg's writing and maintains the dramatic line better than Boulez, and his recordings of the two works tower above all others. The voices on his *Wozzeck* are not the finest on records, but they respond to Boulez as well they should. In the complete *Lulu* Stratas is incomparable—unchallengeable among today's singers in any music of high neurotic content. (Those who saw her *Salomé* on a PBS broadcast from a German production might well ask why Stratas hasn't recorded that opera.)

There is a Pierre Boulez-conducted *Pelléas et Mélisande* (on Columbia), but the singing is inferior, and the opera suffers, despite the marvelous strength in the conducting. The late Eugene Ansermet knew this music as well as any man, and the eloquence of his performance with the ravishing Pelléas of the veteran Mauranne, makes this the recording of choice. It might be noted, however, that there is room for a better *Pelléas* than any now available.

Of and for the People

Bedrich Smetana *(1824-1884)*

The Bartered Bride, *opera in three acts; text by Karel Sabina. First performance, Prague, May 1866*

Modest Mussorgsky *(1839-1881)*

Boris Godunov, *opera in a prologue and four acts; text by Mussorgsky after Alexander Pushkin's drama. First performance, St. Petersburg, February 1874; first performance, revised version, St. Petersburg, February 1896*

Peter Ilyitch Tchaikovsky *(1840-1893)*

Pique Dame, *opera in three acts; text by Peter and Modest Tchaikovsky after Alexander Pushkin's drama. First performance, St. Petersburg, December 1890.*

Serge Prokofiev *(1891-1953)*

War and Peace, *opera in two parts, thirteen scenes; text by Serge Prokofiev and Mira Mendelson after Tolstoy. First performance, Moscow, June 1945*

An obsession with nationality was never far from the thoughts of any composer of Romantic opera. Wagner made no secret that his art was dedicated to a re-establishment of "the holy German art"; Verdi saw to it that his operas, especially the broad, flamboyant early works, made clear the analogy between the fates of the downtrodden—for example the biblical Israelites—and the sufferings of Italy under Austrian rule. A retrieval of national identity was the dominant political mood throughout Europe for most of the nineteenth century, and the arts became the spearhead in proclaiming nationality to a nation's people and to the outside world.

To the East, the lands we now know as Czechoslovakia and the Soviet Union had always had a cultural life, but much of it was imported in an attempt to join the European mainstream. By the 1850s, however, that current had been reversed. In Russia, a group of composers calling themselves "The Five" banded together to bring to serious music an indigenous national accent. In Bohemia, the ardent patriot Bedrich Smetana did the same in his pictorial tone-poems called, simply, *My Country* and in a series of operas both comic and heroic, of which the

Bedrich Smetana

Boris Godunov

sparkling *The Bartered Bride* is by far the best-known.

The Bartered Bride is folk comedy, along a line that extends back to the low comedy of Plautus in ancient times and ahead to the *Fiddler on the Roof* of today. Its hero and heroine are nobody but simple Hans and Marie; there is a marriage-broker to instigate the plot complications, a booby, a circus parade (with trained bear) and, most of all, dancing. The work beguiles its audience with the best-known of Bohemian dances, and even the arias themselves are hardly innocent of dance rhythms. If Smetana's lovely little comedy is the flip side of Wagner's proclamation of nationality through music, it is even farther from Wagner's dictum about music as an art enshrined. *The Bartered Bride* was written to entertain, to charm, and it does so with high skill.

There had been Russian opera before Mussorgksy's *Boris Godunov*. Mikhail Glinka had, in the time of Bellini, studied in Italy and came home to write Russian-language bel canto operas with a few native touches for color but largely under Italian influence. It was the flawed masterpiece of Mussorgsky, however, that gave Russian opera its first widespread expression. Like his colleagues, Mussorgsky never polished his musical training. His setting of scenes from Pushkin's epic drama lacks a consistent dramatic line, and there are scenes that lose themselves, simply because the composer never learned to end a thought properly. However, there is so much raw power in *Boris*—in its portrayal of the central character, the fear-racked usurper, and in its panorama of native character surrounding him—that a night spent in its presence is not soon forgotten. The very sprawlingness of the opera, with its patched-together scenes (including a romantic interlude added after the premiere to make the work more an "opera"), takes on the sweep of all Russian literature; the stunning range of orchestral and choral color seems like a medieval mosaic come to life.

Mussorgsky drew somewhat upon actual Russian folk music in his score, as in his other operas (notably the comedy *Fair at Sorochinsk* which, like *Boris*, was left in need of further editing). One tune, in fact, which is sent to a mighty climax in the brilliant scene of Boris's coronation, had appeared once before, in a quartet that Beethoven had dedicated to the Russian ambassador to Vienna Count Rasoumovsky. More important in *Boris* is that even the original music has the tread and the cadence of Russian folksong, the harmonic rudeness, the changes of rhythm. Some of this rough-cut quality was sandpapered off in Rimsky's revision, to the music's loss. In its pristine state, it is the excelsis of nationalistic opera.

Peter Ilyich Tchaikovsky

Peter Ilyitch Tchaikovsky was not directly identified with the Russian nationalists: his training was considerably more sophisticated, and he achieved international fame before most of his countrymen. Yet his two finest operas are purely Russian: both are settings of Pushkin—the lyric romance *Eugene Onegin* and an even greater work, the stunning supernatural drama *Pique Dame.*

Pushkin's drama, set in an eighteenth-century Moscow of elegance and reverence for the art of its time, drew from Tchaikovsky many kinds of music in which he excelled: music evocative of earlier times, along with soaring lyrical evocations of the love for the hapless Lisa and the obsessive gambler who betrays her. The wonder of *Pique Dame* is Tchaikovsky's command over a blazing range of musical drama. The plot had everything in it to bring out the composer's best: charming, pastoral set pieces evocative of French rococo; a grand ballroom scene; intensely brooding, tragic psychological landscapes all done in musical grayness.

The line of romantic Russian nationalistic drama embraces one masterwork of our own time as well. Serge Prokofiev had left Russia around the time of the 1917 Revolution, and as an exile he had made his mark in music of icy, brilliant virtuosity coupled with a certain modernistic bravado. In this vein he composed—for the Chicago Opera, to be sure—a diabolical setting of Gozzi's ironic comedy *Love for Three Oranges.* But in the 1930s Prokofiev returned to Russia, where he was often obliged to temper his style to conform with the Soviet definition of art. Nevertheless, within this definition, and under the shadow of Hitler's invading armies, Prokofiev achieved a remarkably keen musical mirroring of the immense expanse of Tolstoy's *War and Peace.* Of course the opera, which was patched together for a complete performance only after Prokofiev's death, could use very little of the novel; yet the thirteen scenes selected portray with great skill the expanse of Russia's great defenses against Napoleon and the society that had to be destroyed to make victory possible. The depiction of that society—largely through a series of glistening, slithering waltz tunes—ranks among Prokofiev's keenest dramatic music. The opera requires tremendous stage resources and is therefore seldom mounted—an enormous loss.

Selected Recordings

The Bartered Bride
Zdenek Chalabala and the Chorus and Orchestra of the Prague National Opera *(Pinnacle/Supraphon)*

Boris Godunov
(original orchestration) Martti Talvela, Nicolai Gedda, and Bozena Kinasz, with Jerzy Semkow and the Polish National Radio Chorus and Orchestra *(Angel/EMI)*

(Rimsky-Korsakov version) Nicolai Ghiaurov, Ludovico Spiess, and Galina Vishnevskaya, with Herbert von Karajan and the Sofia Radio Choir and Vienna Philharmonic Orchestra *(London/Decca)*

Pique Dame
Galina Vishnevskaya, Regina Resnik, and Peter Gougaloff, with Mstislav Rostropovitch and French National Chorus and Orchestra *(Deutsche Grammophon)*

War and Peace
Ensemble and Orchestra of the Bolshoi Theater conducted by Alexsander Melik-Pashayev *(Columbia/Melodiya)*

The notion that a composer's music is best handled by his co-nationals breaks down more often than not, but there is indeed a spirit in the Czech version of *The Bartered Bride* that other performances, even with superior casts, cannot quite match. Part of this has to do with the Czech language itself, which, even to someone who doesn't know a word of it, simply *sounds* right—for comedy (as in the patter songs of Eduard Haken as the marriage broker) and for love-making.

Purists will contend that the reorchestration of *Boris Godunov* made after Mussorgsky's death by Nicolai Rimsky-Korsakov smooths out and sentimentalizes the music. Unfortunately, the question becomes rather academic where recordings are concerned. Semkow's performance of the composer's original orchestration does preserve the irregular phrase lengths and slashing orchestral colors, but at some cost. The conducting is dull and spiritless, and the Boris of Martti Talvela—visually so overpowering in the opera house—comes off on records like a series of barks vaguely but only shakily related to pitches. Thus, the "corrupt" Rimsky-Korsakov version under Karajan, with the majesty of Ghiaurov's Boris, has no real competition.

The Rostropovitch recording of *Pique Dame* is a splendid achievement, far superior to older versions once available. The tempos tend to be slow, but on second hearing there is a brooding, massive quality to this performance, abetted by excellent singing, that brings the opera fully to life. As for the Bolshoi Theater's *War and Peace*, it is merely an adequate, somewhat stately run-through, powerfully recorded. The opera being what it is, and as rare as it is, the recording should be acquired as, at least, better than none at all.

Supplementary Recordings

HUMPERDINCK, Engelbert *(1854–1921)*
Hansel and Gretel
Brigitte Fassbaender, Lucia Popp, and Anny Schlemm, with Georg Solti and the Vienna Boys' Choir and Vienna Philharmonic Orchestra *(London/Decca)*
POULENC, Francis *(1899–1963)*
The Dialogues of the Carmelites
Denise Duval, Regine Crespin, and Rita Gorr, with Pierre Dervaux and the French National Opera Chorus and Orchestra *(Angel/EMI)*
JANACEK, Leos *(1854–1928)*
Katya Kabanova
Drakhomira Tikhalova and Benno Blachut, with Jaroslav Krombholc and the Prague National Opera Chorus and Orchestra *(Pinnacle/Supraphon)*
BORODIN, Alexsander *(1833–1887)*
Prince Igor
Oscar Danon and the Ensemble and Orchestra of the Belgrade National Opera *(London/Decca)*

Humperdinck was an ardent Wagnerian, and there is something absurd on appearance about his attempt to adapt his thick, intensely sentimental, densely scored style to a telling of the Brothers Grimm's simple fairy tale. Yet these words are a straw in the wind: *Hansel and Gretel* is nevertheless one of the most popular of operas. At least, hear it in the stylistically accurate Solti performance, in which the German text sounds less embarrassing than the usual English translations.

After a lifetime of composing elegant, witty, cheekily eclectic music—ballets, songs and dances, mostly—Francis Poulenc's style took a serious turn, and his *Carmelites* is beyond doubt his masterpiece. The story is unpromising: the massacre, during the Reign of Terror in France (1793–94), of a group of French nuns at Compiègne and the private story of one of their number. Yet Poulenc, drawing (as he admitted) on the inspiration of Debussy, Mussorgsky, and Monteverdi, fashioned a radiantly beautiful musical setting. Given the staging currently in the Metropolitan Opera repertory—the simplest of movement on an almost bare stage—the opera leaves an audience moved almost beyond tears, and this most stylish recorded performance bears further testimonial to the piercing beauty of the remarkable score.

The Moravian Janacek is only now being discovered in the West, although his early opera *Jenufa*—a violent, romantic plot somewhat akin to some of the Italian *verismo* operas—was for a time the most popular opera of the century. The later opera *Katya Kabanova,* a setting of Alexander Ostrovsky's *The Storm,* is a glowing, romantic work, another of those understated masterpieces that come back to haunt the listener hours later. There is a newer German performance (on London), but this one, in the composer's own language, is stylistically superior.

Prince Igor is Russia's "other" great, flawed, sprawling nationalistic masterwork. It is somewhat like *Boris Godunov* in its episodic, helter-skelter organization but is interesting on its own for its infusion of quasi-oriental coloration. You surely know the Polovtsian Dances from *Prince Igor,* but that is not the only music worth hearing in this extremely well-conceived opera.

5.
Opera Today: Many Directions

In the fall of 1961, the Ford Foundation, which of all American philanthropic sources at the time was the most active in underwriting the arts, began a multi-million-dollar operatic program for the commissioning and staging of new American works. Over a dozen large-scale operas eventuated from the program over the next ten years, mounted by almost every one of America's major opera companies—the New York City Opera and the Metropolitan, the Chicago Lyric and the San Francisco Opera. Not one of these operas, however, has entered the repertory either in its own country or abroad.

Does this necessarily indicate that operatic composition has stopped dead in its tracks? Not necessarily. The failure of the Ford program—the failure, for that matter, of all but a handful of new operas composed anywhere in the world to gain a toehold—is, as much as anything, a reflection of the notion that the world just may have forgotten what opera is.

Let us look at the situation a century or so ago. Europe was an operatic hotbed, and several of America's largest cities had thriving lyric stages as well. The variety of opera was staggering. Italy consumed the throbbing dramatic scores of Verdi as fast as he could turn them out, and there were a few Verdi disciples who were getting an occasional hearing, too. Germany was in the throes of Wagnerism, and some of its houses were also importing the Italian product to the delight—perhaps even relief—of their audiences.

France had its *Carmen* and *Manon* to attract the crowds for a good weepy drama; down the street from the Paris Opéra, there was a fine repertory of more light-weight works by Jacques Offenbach and his cohorts. A light-opera craze also swept over Vienna, thanks to the magnificent flights of fancy by Johann Strauss. In Britain there was the wealth of choice in the eclectic London houses, which offered starry seasons of the best from Germany and Italy while the killingly funny and accurate repertory of Gilbert and Sullivan devastated the serious repertory with its barbed parody. The point is: in all these centers, America included, the taste ran to the latest score—just off the presses, just off the boat. Opera was everybody's musical theater, and it came in all sizes, all emotions.

Today there has been a polarization. The most flourishing opera centers around a repertory hermetically sealed from any infusion of fresh air. The major houses, with exceptions so few as to merit little attention, produce operas chosen from a list that is cut off just about at *Der Rosenkavalier* of 1911. That fact is so well-known, even among composers, that when the Ford Foundation's money was announced as an inducement to producing opera at major houses, every composer went home and wrote a brand-new opera in the style of Puccini. Since their efforts didn't even come out as good Puccini, the results of all of Ford's money merely joined the ill-conceived Edsel car on the discard heap.

The notion—held not only in the United States, but wherever opera is produced at exorbitant costs—that *opera* must always mean grand opera as it existed around 1900 has drastically reduced the fervor for exploration that illuminated the operatic scene a century ago. Yet the operatic world since the end of the First World War has been admirably active, considering the odds.

Peter Grimes

In some cases, the operatic exploration has gone on with both cognizance and affection toward the musical past. England's Benjamin Britten, certainly the most prolific of major operatic composers in this century, made his first mark with the 1946 *Peter Grimes*. It is a large-scale work, intensely romantic in its musical language, its robust choral writing and its dark-hued orchestral sea-scapes full of obeisances to both Debussy and Mussorgsky; its fluent management of an English text is a tribute to Britten's own high literacy. *Grimes* enjoyed a fine success, due in no small measure to the work itself, but also due, possibly, to its emergence in an England of 1946 filled with hope for a rebuilding that would be as much spiritual as structural. Surely Britten was shrewd enough to hold onto his luck. He never again wrote a "big" work but operated instead with fine skill in the realm of chamber opera, spinning off on the way some works of lasting quality—notably, a setting of Andre Obey's *The Rape of Lucretia* and a splendid, gloom-haunted version of Henry James's *The Turn of the Screw.*

Yet the Italian-American Gian Carlo Menotti, who worked at just about the same point as Britten did on the progressive-conservative spectrum, earned none of the respect that the Britisher garnered. Menotti was, to be sure, something of a Puccini clone, although he had better insight into his predecessor's uncanny theatricality than did most of the latter-day imitators. Menotti's real problem was that he was trapped in a situation entirely artificial, an uncertainty as to whether he belonged in the opera house or the musical theater. His most successful works—*The Medium* in 1946 and *The Consul* in 1951—were first produced on Broadway, where they suffered from the average theatergoer's unreasoning dread of "opera" as something effete and abstruse. Later, as a composer with some entrée into opera houses, he again found himself damned—this time, by the intellectuals, who scorned the work of anyone who had written for Broadway.

It could very well be, therefore, that the major impediment to opera today is a failure of definition, the sudden appearance of a totally artificial wall to separate the "serious" art from the "popular." Mozart, Rossini, Meyerbeer, and Verdi would have laughed themselves silly at such an artificial barrier: they were, purely and simply, the best serious composers writing the best popular musical theater of the day. Their enshrinement as "masters" is merely the consequence of their being dead so long.

It can be argued, therefore, that there is more new opera around than most people realize—in the form of the musical theater of today in its more substantial manifestations. The assumption is dangerous in only one respect: the costs of major theatrical production today, coupled with a lingering fear of—or suspicion toward—newness in language and form make it difficult to imagine a splendid new work taking hold in the way Mozart's and Verdi's did in their time.

Yet it happens. George Gershwin, obsessed perhaps to the point of impracticality with the idea of welding his own song style to serious musical forms in the name of American artistic language, created his *Porgy and Bess* as a Broadway opera in 1935. True, it ran to heavy losses then, but in revivals during the 1950s (in a somewhat simplified form), it gradually gained the recognition it enjoys today. The fact that this happened has made it just a little easier for later composers who choose to take Broadway seriously. The case of Stephen Sondheim is an encouraging illustration. Not that, at this writing, his striking, complex kind of musical theater has enjoyed a real money-making run, but at least an interested, questing audience comes. At the great intellectual success of Sondheim's *Sweeney Todd*, a musical setting of a *Grand Guignol* certainly removed from the basic show-biz musical plot, the buzzing around New York was that Sondheim had written an "opera"—meaning, of course, that he had written a work with tunes that are hard to remember and with musical scenes that went on for longer than four minutes at a time.

That was 1979. Nearly forty years before, Kurt Weill had also written long scenes in Broadway shows: a complex interweaving of song material in *Lady in the Dark* that ran

George Gershwin   Kurt Weill

for over fifteen minutes; an "aria" in *Street Scene* lasting twelve. Weill's career, which began in Berlin in the 1920s and was necessarily shifted to New York after Hitler, is a fascinating study in why our operatic outlook lacks a workable set of definitions. In Germany he had begun as a "serious" composer, earning some success with two satirical short operas as well as a great deal of chamber and vocal music. In 1927 came the phenomenal success of *Three-Penny Opera,* for which, inspired by Bertolt Brecht's slangy, folkish text, Weill used a jazz band and wrote in a style into which jazz rhythms intruded. In 1930 Weill and Brecht wrote a work of even greater extent, the satirical-socialist *Rise and Fall of the City of Mahagonny,* jazz-tinged in its language but demanding the production facilities of an opera house.

Yet Weill had no difficulty in recognizing Broadway as his proper milieu upon arriving in America. Today both his German *Mahagonny* and several of his American shows *(Lost in the Stars, Street Scene)* figure in operatic repertories. It seems like wasted effort to consider whether or not this cross-feeding is proper. It is one of the few signs of vitality in the realm of musical drama—by any name—today.

Opera, in the sense of large-scale, abstruse musical drama, does, of course, continue. Some of it even finds its way to records—at least when the signs are propitious. The German Aribert Reimann's *Lear,* an immensely noisy, percussive setting of Shakespeare's tragedy has circulated, thanks in no small measure to its having been written for Dietrich Fischer-Dieskau. At an even farther outpost of the expressive art is *Einstein on the Beach,* a creation of Philip Glass and Robert Wilson running rather a sizable number of hours. It employs electronic means for both its musical and visual aspects and has an attitude toward dramatic line, the management of time, and what constitutes dancing, singing, or playing that might raise an eyebrow among the artistically conservative. Despite all this, the work casts its spell. Opera? Musical drama? Some new form as yet unnamed? It might, in fact, be one or the other. Does it matter? Not so long as it fills a theater with the sense of excitement that has been experienced all over the world since 1607, when Claudio Monteverdi introduced his *Orfeo* in Mantua.

Selected Recordings

SULLIVAN, Arthur *(1842–1900)*
  The Yeomen of the Guard (text by William S. Gilbert)
  D'Oyly Carte Opera Company *(London/Decca)*
OFFENBACH, Jacques *(1819–1880)*
  La Perichole
  Regine Crespin, Alain Vanzo, and Jules Bastin, with Alain Lombard and the Strasbourg Philharmonic *(RCA)*
STRAUSS, Johann II *(1825–1899)*
  Die Fledermaus
  Anneliese Rothenberger, Renate Holm, Brigitte Fassbaender, Nicolai Gedda, and Dietrich Fischer-Dieskau,

with Willi Boskovsky and the Vienna Philharmonic Orchestra *(Angel/EMI)*

MOORE, Douglas *(1893-1969)*
The Ballad of Baby Doe
Beverly Sills, Frances Bible, and Walter Cassel, with Emerson Buckley and the New York City Opera Company Chorus and Orchestra *(Deutsche Grammophon)*

BRITTEN, Benjamin *(1913-1976)*
Peter Grimes
Jon Vickers, Heather Harper, and Jonathan Summers, with Colin Davis and the Royal Opera House Chorus and Orchestra *(Philips)*
The Rape of Lucretia
Janet Baker, Heather Harper, Peter Pears, and Benjamin Luxon, with Benjamin Britten and the English Chamber Orchestra *(London/Decca)*

GERSHWIN, George *(1898-1937)*
Porgy and Bess
Clamma Dale, Donnie Ray Albert, and Larry Marshall, with John DeMain and the Houston Grand Opera Chorus and Orchestra *(RCA)*
(Selections) Leontyne Price and William Warfield, with Skitch Henderson conducting an orchestra *(RCA)*

WEILL, Kurt *(1900-1950)*
The Three-Penny Opera
Frankfurt Opera Ensemble, conducted by Wolfgang Rennert *(Fontana-Philips)*
The Rise and Fall of the City of Mahagonny
Lotte Lenya, Gisela Litz, and Heinz Sauerbaum, with Wilhelm Brückner-Rüggeberg and the North German Radio Chorus and Orchestra *(Columbia/CBS)*
Lady in the Dark (selections)
Gertrude Lawrence *(RCA)*

REIMANN, Aribert *(1936-   )*
Lear
Dietrich Fischer-Dieskau, Julia Varady, and the Ensemble of the Bavarian State Opera *(Deutsche Grammophon)*

GLASS, Philip *(1937-   )* and **WILSON, Robert** *(1944-   )*
Einstein on the Beach
Lucinda Childs, speaker and singer, Vocal and Instrumental Ensemble with Electronic Sounds, and the Philip Glass Ensemble *(Tomato)*

The range in this final record list is vast, from the exquisite craftsmanship of the pure entertainment music from London, Paris, and Vienna in the late nineteenth century to a strange and hypnotic stage piece that might well point the way to the early twenty-first. Yet the operettas of Gilbert and Sullivan, Offenbach, and Strauss—especially in the elements of musical and dramatic satire with which they attempted to puncture the profound silliness of the serious opera of their times—stand at the threshold of one of the vital developments of our own century, the growth of musical theater.

In these works first, then in the slangy, rich vernacular of the vicious, bitter German scores that Kurt Weill created with Bertolt Brecht, and finally in the flawed but terribly earnest attempt by George Gershwin to bring opera to Broadway (or vice versa), the message is clear that there are many ways to put music and words together and to create from their mixture an art form that is higher than each individually. That isn't a new concept; we have seen it throughout this survey. The two recordings of *Porgy and Bess*—the one virtually complete as originally written, the other more in the style of the usual commercial theater productions today (although sung by two supreme operatic personalities)—illustrate interestingly the way this vital if imperfect work does bounce around in our consciousness.

Then there is Britten, who worked at the far edge of the thrust of operatic tradition, a composer who studied his past and made it work once again. *Grimes,* a grand, intense, romantic work, now holds no fears for operatic producers and audiences and is the most recent opera to enter the standard repertory. The Davis performance replaces one of noble manner conducted by Britten himself, but the voice of Jon Vickers so brilliantly reflects the tragedy of Grimes that it must take precedence. *Lucretia* is an even more original masterpiece—brilliant, sardonic, delicate and memorable. The form here is classic: a "chorus" of two singers frames the action and comments on it; the ancient story of Lucretia's downfall is told as if on a sculpture bas-relief. The orchestra is tiny in size but immense in impact.

In a sense, the recent *Lear* of Reimann is also in the same tradition. Its text, drastically cut down from Shakespeare's own, still manages to convey a great deal of the story; its music, largely a whirring, pounding background of percussive sounds, expostulations from brass and various kinds of effects to underline the desolation of the story, still attempts what Mozart and the Romantics attempted in their view of opera—to restore to the total stage work what the libretto was forced to elide or omit.

Finally, there is the strange collaboration between the avant-garde musician Philip Glass and the avant-garde theater creator Robert Wilson. *Einstein* is a vast allegory that does indeed deal in an impressionistic way with the formulator of e = mc², but the dealing is by indirection. The music is made up of repetitions, to the point where it seems to destroy the sense of time itself (or, at least, to challenge it, as Einstein did). In the theater, the power of the cruelly slow evolution of sight and sound in this opera irritated some people, but it fascinated many others. Then,

Einstein on the Beach

for the recording, the work was newly rethought, so that the version without the visuals still has an integrity that differs from the usual fact that a recorded opera is necessarily an incomplete experience. In other words, *Einstein on the Beach,* on records, is in itself an original piece of music, born and maintained on a stage created by the electronic texture of your own amplifier, staged in the space between your own two ears as you listen. Perhaps that is the ideal setting for the opera of the future—a totally personal, even solitary, experience of music-drama, theater without a stage.

A list of Operas by composers mentioned in the text:

BEETHOVEN, Ludwig van
Fidelio, first performance,   1805; revised 1806 and 1814

BELLINI, Vincenzo
Adelson e Salvina,   1825
Bianca e Fernando,   1825
Il Pirata,   1827
La Straniera,   1829
Zaira,   1829
I Capuleti ed i Montecchi,   1830
La Sonnambula,   1830
Norma,   1830
Beatrice di Tenda,   1833
I Puritani,   1833

BERG, Alban
Wozzeck,   1917–21
Lulu,   1928–34

BERLIOZ, Hector
Benvenuto Cellini,   1838
La damnation de Faust (adapted by Raoul Gunsbourg
    1893),   1846
Les Troyens,   1856–59
Béatrice et Bénédict,   1862

BIZET, Georges
La Prêtresse,   1854
Le Docteur Miracle,   1857
Don Procopio,   1859
The Pearl Fishers,   1863
Ivan the Terrible,   1865
The Fair Maid of Perth,   1867
Djarmileh,   1872
Carmen,   1875

BRITTEN, Benjamin
Paul Bunyan,   1940; revised, 1974
Peter Grimes,   1945
The Rape of Lucretia,   1946
Albert Herring,   1947
The Beggar's Opera,   1948
The Little Sweep (one act of *Let's Make an Opera*),   1949

Billy Budd,   1951
Gloriana,   1953
The Turn of the Screw,   1954
Noye's Fludde,   1958
A Midsummer Night's Dream,   1960
Curlew River,   1964
The Burning Fiery Furnace,   1966
The Prodigal Son,   1968
Owen Wingrave,   1970
Death in Venice,   1973

DEBUSSY, Claude
Rodrigue et Chimène (unfinished),   1891
Pelléas et Mélisande,   1902
The Fall of the House of Usher (libretto and vocal score,
   unfinished, 1908–10),   1908

DONIZETTI, Gaetano
Anna Bolena,   1830
L'Elisir d'Amore,   1832
Lucrezia Borgia,   1833
Rosmonda d'Inghilterra,   1834
Maria Stuarda,   1834
Lucia di Lammermoor,   1835
Roberto Devereux,   1837
La Favorita,   1840
La Fille du régiment,   1840
Linda de Chamounix,   1842
Maria de Rohan,   1843
Don Pasquale,   1843
Don Sebastien,   1843
Donizetti wrote over sixty operas.

GERSHWIN, George
Porgy and Bess,   1935

GLASS, Philip
Einstein on the Beach (with Robert Wilson),   1976
Satyagraha,   1977–80

GLUCK, Christoph Willibald (von)
Artaserse,   1741
Demetrio,   1742
Il Tigrane,   1743
Ippolito,   1745
Artmene,   1746
Le Nozze d'Ercole e d'Ebe,   1747

Ezio,   1750
Issipile,   1752
Les Amours champêtres,   1755
Antigono,   1756
Le Chinois poli en France,   1756
L'Isle de Merlin, ou, le Monde renversé,   1758
L'Arbe enchanté,   1759
La Cadi dupé,   1761
Orfeo ed Euridice,   1762
Poro,   1764
La Rencontre imprévue,   1764
Alkestis (Alceste),   1767
Paride ed Elena,   1770
Iphigénie en Aulide,   1774
Armide,   1777
Iphigénie en Tauride,   1779

HANDEL, George Frideric
Rodrigo,   c.1707
Rinaldo,   1711
Il pastor fido, first version,   1712; second and third
   versions,   1733
Teseo,   1713
Amadigi de Gaule,   1715
Acis and Galatea,   c.1718
Radamisto,   c.1720
Floridante,   1721
Ottone,   1723
Giulio Cesare,   1724
Rodelinda,   1725
Admeto,   1727
Tolomeo,   1728
Sosarme,   1732
Ezio,   1732
Orlando,   1733
Arianna,   1734
Alcina,   1735
Atalanta,   1736
Berenice,   1737
Xerxes,   1738
Handel also wrote several lesser operas, many oratorios,
   and other vocal music.

LEONCAVALLO, Ruggiero
I Pagliacci,   1892
La Bohème,   1894
Zaza,   1900

MASCAGNI, Pietro
Cavalleria Rusticana,   1890
L'Amico Fritz,   1891
I Rantzau,   1892
Guglielmo Ratcliff,   1895
Silvano,   1895
Zanetto,   1896
Iris,   1898
Le Maschera,   1901
Amica,   1905
Isabeau,   1911
Parisina,   1913
Lodoletta,   1917
Si,   1919
Il Piccolo Marat,   1921
Pinotta,   1932
Nero,   1935

MASSENET, Jules
Le Roi de Lahore,   1877
Hérodiade,   1881
Manon,   1884
Le Cid,   1885
Werther,   1892
Thais,   1894
La Navarraise,   1894
Cendrillon,   1899
Le Jongleur de Notre Dame,   1902
Don Quixote,   1910

MEYERBEER, Giacomo
Robert le diable,   1831
Les Huguenots,   1836
Le Prophète,   1849
L'Etoile du nord,   1854
Dinorah,   1859
L'Africaine, posthumous first performance,   1865

MONTEVERDI, Claudio
L'Orfeo, first performance,   1607
L'Arianna, first performance,   1608
La Maddalena,   1617
Il combattimento di Tancredi e Clorinda,   1624
Armida,   1627
Mercurio e Marte,   1628
Il ritorno d'Ulisse in patria,   1641
L'Incoronazione di Poppea,   1642

MOORE, Douglas
White Wings, 1935
The Headless Horseman, 1936
The Devil and Daniel Webster, 1939
The Emperor's New Clothes, 1948
Giants in the Earth, 1950
The Ballad of Baby Doe, 1956
Wings of the Dove, 1961
Carry Nation, 1966

MOZART, Wolfgang Amadeus
Bastien und Bastienne, 1768
La Finta semplice, 1769
La Finta giardiniera, 1775
Il re pastore, 1775
Idomeneo, 1781
Il Seraglio (Die Entführung aus dem Serail), 1782
Impresario, 1786
Le Nozze di Figaro, 1786
Don Giovanni, 1787
Così fan tutte, 1790
La Clemenza di Tito, 1791
Die Zauberflöte, 1791

MUSSORGSKY, Modest
Zenitha (The Marriage), performed privately, 1868
Boris Godunov, first version, 1869; rewritten 1872
Kovantshchina, 1872
Fair at Sorochinsk, 1874

OFFENBACH, Jacques
Le Mariage aux lanternes, 1853
Orpheus in the Underworld, 1858
La Belle Hélène, 1864
Bluebeard, 1866
La Vie parisienne, 1866
La Grande Duchesse de Gérolstein, 1867
La Perichole, 1868
Madame Favart, 1878
The Tales of Hoffman, posthumous first performance,
 1881

PEPUSCH, John Christopher, and John Gay
The Beggar's Opera, 1728

PROKOFIEV, Serge
Magdalene, 1911–13
The Gambler, 1915
The Love for Three Oranges, 1919
The Fiery Angel, 1919–27
Simeon Kotko, 1939
The Duenna, 1940
War and Peace, 1941
The Story of a Real Man, 1947

PUCCINI, Giacomo
Le Villi, 1884
Edgar, 1889
Manon Lescaut, 1893
La Bohème, 1896
Tosca, 1900
Madama Butterfly, 1904
The Girl of the Golden West (*La Fanciulla del West*),
   1910
La Rondine, 1917
Il Trittico (*Suor Angelica, Il Tabarro,* and *Gianni
   Schicchi*), 1918
Turandot, posthumous first performance, 1926

PURCELL, Henry
Dido and Aeneas, 1689
The Prophetess or *The History of Dioclesian,* 1690
King Arthur or *The British Worthy,* 1691
The Fairy Queen, 1692
The Indian Queen, 1695
The Tempest or *The Enchanted Island,* 1695

RAMEAU, Jean
Hippolyte et Aricie, 1733
Les Indes galantes, 1735
Castor et Pollux, 1737
Dardanus, 1739
Les Paladins, 1760
Rameau wrote over twenty operas and opera-ballets.

REIMANN, Aribert
Melusine, 1971
Lear, 1978

ROSSINI, Gioacchino
La cambiale di matrimonio, 1810
La Scala di seta, 1812

La Pietra del paragone,   1812
L'Italiana in Algeri,   1813
Tancredi,   1813
Il Turco in Italia,   1814
Elisabetta, Regina d'Inghilterra,   1815
Otello,   1816
Il Barbiere di Siviglia,   1816
La Cenerentola,   1817
La Gazza ladra,   1817
Mosè,   1818
Maometto II,   1820
Zelmira,   1822
Semiramide,   1823
Il viaggio a Reims,   1825
Le Siège de Corinthe (French language version of
    Maometto II),   1826
Moise, (French version of *Mosè*),   1827
Compte Ory, first performance,   1828
William Tell,   1829
Rossini also wrote a number of less well-known operas
    that were popular in their day.

SMETANA, Bedrich
The Brandenburgers in Bohemia,   1863
The Bartered Bride,   1866
Dalibor, first performance,   1868
The Two Widows,   1874
The Kiss,   1876
The Secret,   1878
Libuse, first performance,   1881

STRAUSS, Johann II
Indigo und die vierzig Rauber,   1871
Die Fledermaus,   1874
Eine Nacht in Venedig,   1883
Zigeunerbaron,   1885
Simplizius,   1887
Waldmeister,   1895
Wiener Blut,   1899

STRAUSS, Richard
Guntram, first version,   1892–93; revised, 1940
Feuersnot,   1901
Salomé,   1905
Elektra,   1906–08
Der Rosenkavalier,   1909–10
Ariadne auf Naxos,   1912
Die Frau ohne Schatten,   1914

Intermezzo,   1922–23
The Egyptian Helen,   1924–28
Arabella,   1930–32
The Silent Woman,   1935
Der Freidenstag,   1935
Daphne,   1936–37
The Love of Danae (first performed in 1952),   1938–40
Capriccio,   1940–41

SULLIVAN, Sir Arthur
Cox and Box,   1867
The Zoo,   1875
Trial by Jury,   1875
The Sorcerer,   1877
H.M.S. Pinafore,   1878
The Pirates of Penzance,   1880
Patience,   1881
Iolanthe,   1882
Princess Ida,   1884
The Mikado,   1885
Ruddigore,   1887
The Yeomen of the Guard,   1888
The Gondoliers,   1889
Ivanhoe,   1891
Haddon Hall,   1892
Utopia, Ltd.,   1893
The Chieftan,   1895
The Grand Duke,   1896
The Beauty Stone,   1898
The Rose of Persia,   1899
The Emerald Isle (completed posthumously by Sir Edward
   German),   1901

TCHAIKOVSKY, Peter Ilyich
Eugene Onegin,   1879
Joan of Arc (The Maid of Orleans),   1881
Mazeppa,   1884
The Queen of Spades (Pique Dame),   1890
Iolanthe,   1892

VERDI, Giuseppe*
Oberto,   1839
Un Giorno di regno,   1840
Nabucco,   1842
I Lombardi,   1843
Ernani,   1844
I Due Foscari,   1844
Alzira,   1845

---

*Dates given are for first performance of each Verdi opera

Giovanna d'Arco, 1845
Attila, 1846
Macbeth, 1847; revised, 1865
I Masnadieri, 1847
Luisa Miller, 1849
La Battaglia di Legnano, 1849
Rigoletto, 1851
La Traviata, 1853
Il Trovatore, 1853
I Vespri Siciliani, 1855
Aroldo, 1857
Simon Boccanegra, 1857; revised, 1881
Un Ballo in Maschera, 1859
La Forza del Destino, 1862
Don Carlos, 1867
Aida, 1871
Otello, 1887
Falstaff, 1893

WAGNER, Richard * *
Rienzi, 1842
The Flying Dutchman, 1843
Tannhäuser, 1845
Lohengrin, 1851
Tristan und Isolde, 1865
Die Meistersinger, 1868
Das Reingold (part 1 of *Der Ring des Niebelungen*), 1869
Die Walküre (part 2 of *Der Ring des Niebelungen*), 1870
Siegfried (part 3 of *Der Ring des Niebelungen*), 1876
Götterdämmerung (part 4 of *Der Ring des Niebelungen*), 1876
Parsifal, 1882

WEBER, Carl Maria von
Das Walmädchen, 1800
Peter Schmoll und seine Nachbarn, 1801
Abu Hassan, 1811
Der Freischutz, first performance, 1821
Euryanthe, first performance, 1823
Oberon, first performance, 1826

WEILL, Kurt
The Protagonist, 1926
The Three-Penny Opera, 1928
Happy End, 1929
The Rise and Fall of the City of Mahagonny, 1930
Down in the Valley, 1948

**Dates given are for first performance of each Wagner opera

PICTURE CREDITS